# Look Up
## From Your
# Phone
## So I Can Love You

**Amy M. Vannieuwenhoven**

I0584494

**NORTHWESTERN PUBLISHING HOUSE**
Milwaukee, Wisconsin

Cover Artwork: Shutterstock
Interior Artwork: Agata Kuczminska, Good Stuff No Nonsense
Art Director: Karen Knutson
Designer: Lynda Williams

Northwestern Publishing House
1250 N. 113th St., Milwaukee, WI 53226-3284
www.nph.net
© 2018 Northwestern Publishing House
Published 2018
Printed in the United States of America
ISBN 978-0-8100-2915-6

18  19  20  21  22  23  24  25  26  27        10  9  8  7  6  5  4  3  2  1

# Table of Contents

# Why Journal ?

There's no turning back. Most people born into this world from now on will *never* know life without digital technology at their fingertips. As of 2017, 44% of the *world* population (the world being over *7 billion people*) has smartphones—and a predicted 59% of the population will have them by 2022 (Sui). This fact is neither good nor bad; it simply is a reality of life. And, short of some dystopian accident (think of the futuristic books and movies where the common person no longer has access to technology), this is **not** going to change—technology is here to stay.

So . . . forging ahead, as kids and parents, you will need to decide how you are going to navigate this brave new world together *(and since you're reading this, you're not choosing to run away from society and live in a cave . . . yet)*. So why should you journal in order to brave this world together? You maybe haven't ever thought about the facts that you are not just randomly here and that your family is not randomly thrown together. You may have never thought about your family being meant or even destined to face life together, but God placed you together as a family. God knew that as people, we *seek, want,* and *need* other people. We have the natural need to talk and be heard, to show love—and be loved in return. We need to hug and experience physical touch—to *interact with other people*. Basically, we **need** to communicate and care for one another in different ways. As families, we take care of one another's needs.

Again, why should you journal? Journaling gives a flexible way to have that conversation that doesn't always easily happen in "real time." Sometimes schedules keep us from talking—there are jobs, school and extracurricular activities, and of course, *life* (which may include other brothers/sisters/relatives and *their* two cents' worth!). Sometimes we need time to respond (or at least to answer *thoughtfully,* as most of us have had times when we wish we could take back words we said without thinking!). And honestly, some-times it's awkward to start the conversation about these things face-to-face (or maybe even to know *what* we should be having a conversation about). And, no, kids, this is not another way to torture you! This is an opportunity to get to know each other, to communicate, to have parents and kids give ideas about how you are going to spend your time and energy (and yes, use the tech-nology with which we've been blessed). Journaling? Just think of it as texting without your phone *(the phone bill may prove that you can text* 😊*))*.

## Guidelines and Ground Rules

 **1. Decide who is going to see this.** Ideally, this would just be between you, the parent(s), and you, the child. Because you are being honest, you need to decide what is fair to share with others (like the guidelines you decide for technology use or family-only time, etc.). However, that also means that parents don't share personal entries with friends or other children without permission, and vice versa. Honesty is the key, and if you can trust that neither of you will embarrass the other or share personal things about the other (no matter how juicy), that will help keep you both sharing honestly.

*Initial here that you understand* _____
*(or make changes/additions you both agree on):*

_____

_____

_____

_____

_____

_____

 **2. Decide on where/how this journal will pass between you.** You may want to use bedside tables or bedrooms as places to pass the book back and forth (yelling, "Hey, you!" as you chuck the book at each other is not a great option). You might mark how far you should go (or have gone) with a sticky note or bookmark, decide to do a section each week, etc.

*Here is how I would like this journal*
*to be passed back and forth:* _____

_____

_____

_____

_____

 **3. Be patient with each other as you navigate and set boundaries.** Your family is different from any other family that has been or will exist *(and that's not just because you think your sister is weird* 😊*)*. Remember, God chose to put you together (and, by the way, God doesn't make mistakes—that's all I'm saying). There often enough is no right or wrong answer (this isn't math class!), but this book will help your family find good answers. This is a tool to help you look at boundaries and good choices for safety, entertainment, and time management. And, you won't know what works for you (or have the blessings of becoming closer), unless you put in the time to find out!

**I will take the time to *faithfully* journal and *patiently* think about and *consider* what you write.**

*Initial here that you (parent(s) and child) understand (or make changes/additions you both agree on):* _____

_____

_____

_____

_____

 **4. Read how to use this interactive journal.** Within the entire journal, some sections are marked "Kids" and some are marked "Parents." That being said, you should both read each other's sections. Quickie quiz: Which sections should you read? Both! An interactive journal means that different people are adding responses for each other to read, think about, and respond to. You can't fully appreciate what the other is journaling unless you read that section and then see how your parent/child responded. Each section will be written for parents, kids, or both, but the entire book is intended to help you know and appreciate each other better. Also, please understand that some parts of the book aren't specifically about smartphones and screen time, but they're dedicated to helping families simply rediscover each other and grow closer. The better you know each other, the better you can relate, grow closer, and respect each other's viewpoints. When you have finished, the goals are that you will understand each other better, have a plan for how to responsibly use technology, grow in your appreciation for God (who put you together) and each other, and, quite possibly, you might take a little time to look up from your phone so you can love each other even more!

# Anticipated L-O-V-E

*Kids (and Parents too!):*

Remember when you got your first phone? It may have been a hand-me-down from a parent, or you may have researched it, stalked it, and saved for it. No matter how it came to be yours, it was something you looked forward to having—something you anticipated having and using. You probably gathered friends' numbers and usernames before you even had the phone as your own. And when the phone became yours, it was *amazing*. You showed it to all your friends. You took care of it and probably made sure it had a case and screen cover to protect it. You still check it often and take it with you everywhere. You *love* your phone.

*Share your memories of your first phone (or waiting for it, begging for it . . . ):*

*Kids:*_____

_____

_____

_____

*What are some things (events, gadgets, etc.) you are still looking forward to (<u>anticipating</u>):*

*Kids:*_____

_____

_____

_____

_____

Not to upstage your trip down "phone memory lane," but there is another love story that is very similar. It's *yours*. Your parents anticipated (hoped for, dreamed about) you. They studied baby books and medical journals. And when you came, well, you were *amazing*. Your parents took care of you and made sure you had clothes and a ton of baby equipment. They checked on you often (even when you were soundly sleeping, just to make sure you were still fine). They took you *everywhere* and showed you off. They *love* **you**—and who can blame them?

*Parents, share a memory and/or confession of smothering love* 😊: _____

_____

_____

_____

_____

And even greater than phone memories or your parents' anticipation of you is the love of God for you. See, not only did God put you with your family, but he anticipated you and your needs. He knew all of us—mind blown, because that is *a lot* of people. And since God knows us, he also knows we are not perfect. You may be awesome, but you and no one else on the face of the earth is ever perfect, right, A+ every second of the day. And God *knew* that. Because we cannot live perfectly, God sent his Son, Jesus, to earth to live a perfect life for each of us. He anticipated that we would need Jesus. You may have memorized this passage (or seen it on signs or painted on faces at football games): 📖 "For God so loved the world that he gave his one and only Son, that whoever believes in him shall not perish but have eternal life" (John 3:16). God chose to give us life in exchange for his only Son's life—that's true love! That's really amazing to think about—we don't have the option to pick our parents or kids *(as many times as you wish you could have!)*. Sometimes we can pick our phones, but often it's just what the carrier offers, what's cheap, or what hand-me-down you get. But God actually chose to create us, to put us together, and to save us through Jesus! You are special! You are not a whim, a chance coincidence, or the last person left when choosing teams—you are special, chosen and loved!  "Indeed, the very hairs of your head are all numbered" (Luke 12:7)—think about how deeply God *knows* you—down to the last hair! And he keeps providing whatever we need (something we still have left to look forward to—or *anticipate*). God chose to give us *to each other* to navigate through this life. All blessings are from God, but families are an especially needed and special gift—a gift God anticipated us needing. God *loves* **us**.

*Kids and Parents: Share some of the blessings in your life (people/things/pets).*

Kids:_____

_____

_____

_____

_____

Parents:_____

_____

_____

_____

_____

*Kids and Parents: You are an anticipated gift; share with ONE word how this makes you feel:*

Kids:_____

Parents:_____

This is how we know what love is:
Jesus Christ laid down his life for us.
(1 John 3:16)

3

# Connectivity Issues?

**Kids (Parents too):**

Ever had three, maybe even four or five bars of signal on your phone and still not really have a good connection? You keep getting that circulating icon, but it won't fully connect you even though the bars show it should. My family has experienced this while driving through the mountains. We try to use an app or check how far we are from our destination, but the phone won't connect. Suddenly, one person will appear to have a signal or be connecting, only to lose it again. Frustrating!!!! Our relationships can be kind of like this too. We may all go through the normal routine of our lives, and we might look like we're connected. But sometimes we're just like the circulating icon—we're not actually making a connection with each other.

Like a device that refuses to connect, sometimes you have to power down and just start over. So, let's go back and start over with *your* beginning. Just like you'd restart your phone to help it connect, let's "restart" your family's story to help strengthen your connection, starting from your *family's* very beginning.

Your full name:_____

Chosen because/means/named after:_____

_____

_____

Parents' names:_____

_____

4

*Named because or means:*_____

_____

_____

As mentioned before, God even knows how many hairs are on your head! Your parents probably couldn't even count how many *(many, many)* hours they've spent taking care of your sweet little *(at least at one time!)* head. They've smoothed your hair *(washed/cut/picked nits?)*, iced goose eggs, possibly had x-rayed, or simply stared down at your sweet infant head snuggled in sleep.

*Your hair color (and any changes since birth):*_____

_____

*Inherited from? Looks most like this relative/family side:*__

_____

_____

*Parents' hair colors (and changes along the way* 😊*):*

_____

_____

_____

_____

*Inherited from?:*_____

_____

_____

_____

Your parents certainly do love that beautiful head of yours. But it may seem that they're seeing it on more than just old baby pictures from "Throwback Thursdays" on social media. Studies show that kids today are spending more and more time looking down at devices—in fact, more than 7.5 hours a day for 8- to 18-year-olds, and more than 10 hours' worth if they are multitasking (switching between more than one media at a time during those 7.5 hours)! (The Henry J. Kaiser Family Foundation). That is *a lot* of time to just look at your pretty head again—and only the top of it! And, as sweet as it is, parents don't just want to stare at your bent, distracted head; they want to connect *with* you and actually see and connect with your beautiful eyes too!

*Your eye color:*_____

*Inherited from/most like:*_____

_____

*Parents' eye colors:*_____

*Inherited from/most like:*_____

_____

It is said that eyes are the windows to the soul. Now, that's not in a spiritual sense, but our eyes and eye contact do share so much! You can tell if someone you know is *really* smiling or is faking it just by looking at his or her eyes. When you send pictures to friends, you are looking *directly* at the camera. Why is that? We connect with other people through our eyes, through special looks—even glares communicate our intended messages. So if you are possibly spending seven hours a day looking at a screen, you may be missing the human contact with your family that just looking up, making eye contact, and being present can give!

*Kids: How many hours do you think you honestly spend on your phone/media on an average day?*_____

_____
_____

If possible, look at your past phone bill(s). Most bills will detail how many minutes, texts, or data you've used each month. It may shock you—*not in a horror movie way, just possibly in a "your hair in the morning way"* 😊.

*Phone bill reality check (if possible):*

_____

*Kids and Parents:*
Now think about how much time you've spent actively talking and communicating with each other lately. Does your time spent on

your devices vs. your time spent communicating with your family show how much you value the people in your life?

Think about this: A pastor once shared an illustration that might help us understand the value of devices vs. people. If you have a friend, or maybe even a girl- or boyfriend, what do you do? You spend time with him or her. If you don't spend time together or communicate together in some form, your relationship *cannot* grow. In the same way, if you say you love and care about someone, yet you don't really communicate or spend time (*actively* spend time, not just being near each other while doing something else!) with that person, your relationship will not grow—and may even shrink and die.

Taking this to another level, the pastor's point was not just to show how we keep healthy relationships with people but also to show that we need to spend time learning about God (who anticipated and loves us) to have a healthy relationship with him too. We can *say* we have a relationship with God, but if we don't spend time in his Word, then that relationship can't grow either. (If this seems new to you, just keep working through the book together—your family and spiritual relationships will grow as you respond to each other and see your family's and God's love for you!)

**Thinking time:** So, how's my connection with my parents/kids? Do we spend time together (*really* together)? Or are we more like two toddlers at a train table—both playing, but not actually playing with each other (*well, unless you have the train I WANT—and then maybe fighting together?*).

*What do we do—or would we want to do—together?*

*Parents' reflection:*_____

_____

_____

_____

*Kid's reflection:*_____

_____

_____

_____

Sometimes we don't fully connect or treasure something because we truly don't recognize the **value** in what we have. You may have a favorite bracelet or watch from your younger years that you've always liked, but when you find out that it belonged to a grandparent, it seems more special, **more valuable**. Or maybe you had trading cards, and suddenly you realize one is worth a large amount of money. What you had didn't *actually* change, but your view, or perspective, of it has changed now that you know the actual worth.

*What are some things you value (it could be something you own, were given, or even something like time with a friend):*

*Kids:*_____

_____

_____

*Parents:*_____

_____

_____

You probably value having a phone because you know what you can do with it. You may not even realize how much becoming closer (reconnecting) to your parents (and that Savior, Jesus, we've mentioned a few times) may help you realize *their* true value too. Remember how we talked about how much your parents and God anticipated you? You possibly don't think too much about your parents—they're always just there, right? And God? Maybe he hasn't seemed like much more than someone out there keeping the world turning. But as you learn more about your relationship with your family and God, you will see them differently—they will hold a different value for you. (And without your parents and God, you wouldn't even exist . . . so there'd just be this lonely phone lying there 🙁).

We can't have God fill out the same questions you and your parents just did, but we can look at what the Bible says about him and see his value there.

📘 For instance, if you think that God is nice but he's just a being who created you, who smiles down on you, and who is the reason for Christmas and Easter celebrations, you may not see such a treasure in God (other than the holiday gifts and celebrations). You may need to know more about God to see his value. If I tell you that "the Lord made the heavens and the earth, the sea, and all that is in them" (Exodus 20:11), you can see God as an almighty, powerful being. Whether you can create amazing things or *you've been banned from the art room,* you cannot create this whole amazing world and keep it moving with your words. Recognizing God's matchless power can really strengthen your connection to him.

*What is something in this world (God's creation) that you admire?*

Kids:_____

_____

_____

Parents:_____

_____

_____

You have a God "who wants all people to be saved and to come to a knowledge of the truth" (1 Timothy 2:4). This shows a God who loves *all* people and wants them to know his Son, Jesus, who died to pay for all the wrongs that everyone has ever done. You may like most people, but *you* can't save them—only by knowing Jesus (who died that holy death for us) can a person be saved!

You may not have thought much about Jesus dying for all people and wanting them to be saved. Or maybe you've learned about Jesus all your life, but each year you appreciate his love more and more.

*Pick a word (or words) to describe God based on the two paragraphs above.*

Kids:_____

_____

_____

Parents:_____

_____

_____

You also have a God who is available and wants you to seek him out about *anything!* God tells us, "Do not be anxious about anything, but in every situation, by prayer and petition, with thanksgiving, present your requests to God" (Philippians 4:6). God *wants* us to pray to him—to go to him about problems or in times of joy to thank and praise him for all he's given us. No one person is available to help all the time, but God is. You may not have much experience praying, but you've likely had really good times and really bad times (and God loves to hear from us in those times—good, bad, and in-between!). And there's no magic formula to reach him. God hears us no matter how we approach him: with a "Dear God . . . thank you for . . ." or "I'm really struggling with . . . and I know that you said you are here, so can you help guide me through my problems?" Prayers can be out loud or in your head, written down or spur of the moment, and in **any** place or time.

*List something you'd like to thank, praise, or ask for guidance from God about:*

*Kids:*_____

_____

_____

_____

*Parents:*_____

_____

_____

_____

God wants us to spend time in his Word so that our faith in Jesus as our Savior can be strengthened: "Faith comes from hearing the message, and the message is heard through the word about Christ" (Romans 10:17). God wants us to spend time in his Word, getting to know him, seeing his value and love, and praising him. You can reread any other book as much as you want, but it will only help you remember what you already read (or put you to sleep). The Bible actually strengthens your faith when you read it again and again. What a miracle! The Bible tells the most beautiful love story: we were lost, and God found and saved us. You may even feel excited to get to know this awesome God, but, well, you're maybe not sure where to start. Pull out your Bible. Don't have one? Ask for a Bible (I have a free Bible app). Then what??? Talk to Mom and Dad and your pastor—find and underline the passages you read here as a start! Through the Word of God, you can deepen your connection to God, who wants to spend eternity (time in heaven) with you!

*If you have a favorite Bible passage or Bible story, please share. (If you haven't been in a Bible much, see if you can find a favorite in this book and copy it down):*

Kids:_____

_____

_____

_____

Parents:_____

_____

_____

_____

As you explore and deepen your connection with God, you will see that he wants to be first in your life: "You shall have no other gods before me" (Deuteronomy 5:7). God is the one who created us, loves us, and anticipated our needs, so it makes sense that he wants us to praise him before other things. You wouldn't expect your favorite toys from the past to start telling you what to do, and neither do we—the ones God *created*—flip roles with our God. Imagine your favorite stuffed animals telling you how it's going to be from now on . . . a funny picture, but entirely ridiculous. When you see the value of God and realize how much he's doing to care for and love us, it's kind of silly that we think we could tell him how life's going to be. It's also so easy to love the things of this world— not only love for this beautiful land of plenty, but anyone with a TV can see how many things out there compete for our attention! These things compete for our attention and want to edge God out of first place. Anything we love more than God could really become a "god"—something trying to be first in our lives. For adults, it could be wanting more money or things than God has given them.

For kids, it could be the NEED to have the next device or clothes at any cost or the sports that we rearrange our whole lives for.

*What are some of the "things" of this world you see trying to come before God in our human lives?*

*Parents' reflection:*_____

_____

_____

_____

_____

*Kid's reflection:*_____

_____

_____

_____

_____

When we seek to deepen our relationship with God, we also see the things and people in our lives as blessings from God (again, we see value). Parents see children as gifts, and children see parents as gifts. Psalm 127:3 declares, "Children are a heritage from the Lord, offspring a reward from him." That means a child is no longer just a cute little "mini-me," but he or she is a *gift* from *God*. God further encourages parents to deepen their children's connections to the Lord by "[bringing] them up in the training and instruction of the Lord" (Ephesians 6:4).

And for children, God gives a command and promise: "Honor your father and mother, as the Lord your God has commanded you, so that you may live long and that it may go well with you" (Deuteronomy 5:16). (You may want to highlight this section; it's going to come up again and again and maybe again—*and maybe you should make a poster of it—jk—but, well, you could* 😊). God, in his perfect love for us, tells children not just to love their parents but to honor them. "To honor" shows that someone or something deserves a special position of respect and worth. God gives the added promise that those who do this may have a long, blessed life. Who *doesn't* want life to go well?

Explain in your own words the roles of parents and kids from the two previous paragraphs:

Role of parents:

Parents' response: _____

_____

_____

Kid's response: _____

_____

_____

Role of children:

Parents' response: _____

_____

_____

Kid's response: _____

_____

_____

How does all this affect us? Knowing that we have a great God (one I want to grow closer to!) changes how we see the world. We can marvel at what he did to fix our great big disconnect with him—all the wrongs we do that offend him and defy him—how he loved us enough to have his Son pay for all the world's wrongs with his life, his own blood, at the cross. And we learn more and more that we don't need to listen to all the distractions/calls of this world (or we can at least start seeing which ones to mute 😊) because we want to live our lives to thank and value our God.

One picture of thanks to God was seen in the way people worshiped God before Jesus came to earth as our Savior. God had his people offer sacrifices (valuable farm animals burnt up on an altar) to represent that a life (it would later be Jesus' perfect life) needed to be given to pay for all the wrongs they had done (their sins).

Now that Jesus has come to be that sacrificed life, as saved, thankful people, the Bible encourages us (God's children) to live lives of thanks to him: 📖 "Therefore, I urge you, brothers and sisters, in view of God's mercy, to offer your bodies as a living sacrifice, holy and pleasing to God" (Romans 12:1). (Mercy is when you are kind to someone because you see they really need help.) Because of God's mercy in saving us, we now live for him. We don't offer animals, because the perfect sacrifice was already paid in full at Jesus' cross. However, now everything we do can show thanks ("living sacrifices" = "thanksliving"!).

Out of thanks and out of love, we continue to deepen our relationship with God and with each other by spending time with God's Word and each other. When we think of the ultimate gift—that God valued us enough to send Jesus for us—we can start to see everything around us as gifts. We again see God's love in "gifting" us a family, and the more we learn of God, the more we see the honor, love, and value in a family. Like any operating system or app, we may need to "update" from time to time (toddler knowledge of God and our family, upgraded to older child knowledge, *then to teen almost-know-it-all knowledge* ☺), but seeing each other as gifts, as *God's* gifts to each other, makes us **want** to take the time to love and know each other—to reconnect.

**Story Time:** Can you really connect better by remembering the value of other people? Yes. This may shock you, but as a teacher I sometimes deal with discipline problems *(gasp!)*. I very often find that taking the time to gently ask why (why did you do or say that?) and then waiting patiently for the answer helps connect me to those around me (usually my students, but it works with anyone). After waiting—again, patiently—for the disruption to stop, the sheepish apology follows, and then I say the line that I hope they'll remember most. I tell them, "God has been patient and loving with me, and I will also be patient and loving with you." I hope they remember that I am a sinner (not perfect), but I love my God so much that I am willing to go the extra mile to share the patience and love **God** has shown me.

So . . . one day a student needed a "special escort" to the hallway after several reminders to stop tipping backwards on his chair. We looked at each other calmly, and I said, "Can you imagine the phone call I'd have to make to your mother explaining that if *I'd* just held out to be a little *'meaner,'* a little more tough in my love, your son would still be alive?" I'd hardly finished the words and a smile cracked his face. He knew. He knew I wouldn't back down on calling him out when I needed to, and yet I'd be patient with him also because I love him enough—because *I've* been loved that much by God. The value I see in God motivates *(compels)* me to love other people unconditionally and patiently, as I have been loved by God.

I challenge you to see how valuable your God is—especially in his gifts of Jesus, your Savior, and your family!

Christ's love compels us . . .
he died for all, that those who live
should no longer live for themselves
but for him who died for them
and was raised again.
(2 Corinthians 5:14,15)

# Balancing Act

There is a time for everything
and a season for every activity
under the heavens.
Ecclesiastes 3:1

*Kids (and Parents):*

I'm pretty sure you don't wake up and think, "I'm willfully keeping my family from socializing with me today; I'm not really going to honor my parents today, and I'm not going to let God be first in my life either because I'd much rather look at my phone." The problem is that it's just so easy to become distracted by notifications, games, websites, and/or social media.

Don't ban the phone yet or think, *I can't handle where this conversation may go, and let's stop working through this book.* Let's just see how well your family is doing with balancing technology use vs. the hours in a day. We want to deepen our relationship for a better connection, so let's look at the nitty-gritty facts.

Guess how much time you think you (kids) spend in each category on the chart below (fill in the "Time Spent Guesstimate" column) and then keep track as well as you can for an agreed-upon number of days (media use amount is recorded in the previous chapter). Most people (adults included) are realizing in this tech-heavy society that there needs to be some balance between *using devices* and *being present* with people.

*Time period (your choice):*
*week/10 days/month/dates:_____to_____*

| Important Parts of My Life | Time Spent Guesstimate | | Actual Time Spent-ish (totals per week/ 10 days/month/etc.) |
|---|---|---|---|
| | Kids | Parents | |
| Media (nonschool internet, phone, text, mixed media, apps, digital games) | | | |
| With Friends | | | |
| With Parents (meaningfully, not while on a device ☺) | | | |
| Religious Activity (church, personal study, youth group) | | | |
| Playing Sports | | | |
| Awake | | | |
| Asleep | | | |
| Miscellaneous Groups/Activities: | | | |

*React to how the chart turned out.*

*Parents' response:* _____

_____

_____

_____

_____

_____

_____

*Kid's response:* _____

_____

_____

_____

_____

_____

_____

*Parents: Time to ponder.*

⚠ Do you use your phone, tablet, or computer for work and then frequently work at home on it/them too?

⚠ Do you regularly use social media when you are sitting with the family?

⚠ Do you read blogs, surf the internet, or answer texts or emails during family meals?

*Parents: Write about your own tech habits (be honest; you're not being graded!):*

_____

_____

_____

_____

Children are navigating an interesting world.

This tech world is their normal life. Sure, they may have had to wait a *little* bit to get a phone, but they've cut their teeth on computers, tablets, and all sorts of media. They don't need much formal instruction, they have few fears about trying out new technology, and they learn by instinct or trial and error.

All that being said, they take their cues from parents about when or how to do anything. A child who grows up seeing a parent always on a device learns that this is "what we do." Little children bring parents their phones when notifications ring or beep because they recognize that the phone's noises are important to their parents (and get parents' attention). Little children pretend to text and talk on the phone; they are copying their parents. Little children (and bigger children too!) are looking for approval from parents, and they will equate taking Mommy her cell phone with making Mommy happy.

Parents need to be aware of the unintentional messages they may be sending through personal tech habits. We know the saying that actions speak louder than words. Kids who see parents surfing or working on devices may be frustrated when told *they* can't be on a device. To them, this may say, "Do as I say, not as I do." We want to be mindful as parents that we aren't displaying poor examples.

Do we sneak calls in every time we have a few spare seconds? Do we duck out to answer calls or texts—when really they could've waited? It is a balancing act, and as parents, we are the kids' first and main examples of how to responsibly use technology.

Most parents hope that their own kids will want to be, *at least a little bit,* like them someday. What you believe is important will be reflected to your children. Therefore, you probably don't dream for your daughter to want to text like Mom *(and let's face it, your daughter's probably already better—she'd tell you to turn the phone sideways and use your thumbs)*. And dads, you probably won't aim to have your sons surf the internet for the sports facts and funny videos like you might do *(like those racing geese videos—seriously!?)*. But if those things *appear important* to you, then they send a message that these things should be important to your child too.

Parents: Share tech habits and uses you think are a good use of your time:_____

_____

_____

_____

_____

Share tech habits you might want to change or curb:_____

_____

_____

_____

_____

Kid's perspective: "Weigh-in" on your parent's/parents' media habits (How are my parents with tech habits?! This is a no-grounding zone—just be honest 😊):_____

_____

_____

_____

_____

*Parents*:

Now that you, as parents, have started to think about your own tech habits, let's approach another issue. Many parents become frustrated with a child's constant cell phone/device use but may have never **taught** them how to realize what's "too much time" or "just the right amount." Part of the problem is that many in the current parenting generation didn't grow up with this constant connectivity, so you maybe haven't even stopped to think about what "good boundaries" look like. Sure, you may have had a gaming system and a really long-corded telephone, but those things required you to be somewhat within the hearing and seeing distance of everyone. You could not use the phone *for hours on end* because someone else would eventually need to use it. So thinking about boundaries with this kind of technology is a completely new area for many parents to pioneer (in other words, you can't just do what your parents did!). And the kids, well they don't *know* what their boundaries should be because they're *kids!* They're expecting *you* to set the boundaries for them. It isn't fair to scold children about being on media too much if you've never **taught** them what "too much" is. Children will generally assume that what they are doing is fine if you don't address it. So being frustrated and building up like a pressure cooker because *"my kid is always on that device!"* and then exploding could be **scary, hurtful, and confusing** (especially if there may have never been any teaching or guidelines laid!). Your child is likely to become *more* separated from you if that kind of communication (the exploding type) keeps happening. Communicate, communicate.

Humans, in general, are unique in that it takes many more years for them to fully mature than any other living species. God gave children to parents to be trained by them for this life and the next. So before we as parents become upset that this generation "doesn't know common etiquette" and will possibly lack the social skills that previous generations learned, let's stop the frustration and start a dialogue with kids (journal style, and then the actual conversation should be easier to start). Or, the next time you're at one of those restaurants with the color crayons and paper for the tablecloth, start drawing and doodling together—go old school. Or maybe tally who can count the most people on cell phones in the restaurant 😊. Rome wasn't built in a day, but it was beautiful (*as long as you managed to avoid being eaten by lions in the Colosseum*). Your child's skills, habits, etc. are not created or destroyed in one day (well, probably not); you've got some time to work on it.

*Do children know what's too much? Are parents teaching and giving guidelines? Are you teaching and giving guidelines? Give your thoughts or examples.*

*Parents' viewpoint:*_____
_____
_____
_____
_____

*Kid's viewpoint:*_____
_____
_____
_____

**Throwback fun**—Parents: Go back to your childhood. "I remember when . . ." helps connect the generations (what was it you could or couldn't do, the rules you had to follow) and, well, it is just plain funny.

*Any great recollections of the "good ole days"? Corded phones? Favorite games—or what you didn't have that <u>everyone else did</u>?*

_____
_____
_____
_____
_____

*Parents and Kids: Write down ideas of what might be acceptable amounts of time and check back to see how you did on the chart earlier in this chapter compared to what you think is an acceptable balance (and how it would look in your home for <u>both</u> of you!).*

Keep in mind that these family boundaries are often found by trial and error and do often change over time. Preview—this will come in a later chapter also: The American Academy of Pediatrics recommends limiting total screen time to less than two hours a day. Obviously, there are exceptions and differences for usage. The main point is that you realize you want the relationships you value (God, family) to be reflected by the amounts of time you spend on them!

*Parents' ideas for what would be good time limits:*_____

_____

_____

*Kid's ideas for what would be good time limits:*_____

_____

Psst . . . comparing your "acceptable time" ideas over ice cream or a favorite treat might be a fun way to *balance* relationship time together with working together.

Also, this idea of "how much time is good" is really just the beginning of learning life skills. All through life, we need to decide how much time we will spend resting, working, exercising, etc. We've already mentioned that this technology is not going away, so let's think about habits that will be good for the future too. When you, as parents and child, set these goals, think about how you are going to be accountable to keeping them. I frequently set timers on my phone or the microwave to help me remember when to start or stop things. These help me remember anything from when it's clean up/dismissal time at school to "I should take Dad's dress shirt out of the dryer" to that's how much screen time my child has.

*What kind of habits or helps can you think of to help your family be successful now and in the future when you use technology?*

*Parents' ideas:* _____

_____

_____

_____

Kid's ideas:_____

_____

_____

_____

Parents and Kids—more balance . . .

# Tech Time-outs

Tech time-outs are exactly what they sound like—a time-out from technology. This may mean that dinner is not interrupted by any tech device (or any other time that the family decides). During your technology "okay" time, you may WANT to go online and look up some family helps, like family technology contracts. There are even sites dedicated to helping families take a technology time-out (Foresters). There are challenges, like the "Tech Timeout Academic Challenge," available to help kids see if they can last three days without the technology and then see what they had been missing during all that screen time. They are NOT saying throw out the phones, computers, or tablets ✏️ —just *intentionally* unplug for a little while as a way to plug back into each other. Whether through a website's help or your own invention, you can intentionally cut the cord (*not the actual cord, though—THAT would be a huge electrical hazard* 😊 *. . . but it definitely would give you a tech time-out!*).

> *What would be a starting point for where/when to have technology and where/when not to? In other words, what are some reasonable situations where your family could say, "No tech during that"? (Remember—balance):*

Kid's reaction:_____

_____

Parents' reaction:_____

_____

Don't panic if you have to keep readjusting the balance until it feels right (unless, of course, you are my grade school friend who bit through her tongue when the teeter-totter came down too fast—a good reminder to move slowly and deliberately!).

Need some help unplugging? Many of us do. Blogger *(and crafty guy)* Mark Love felt **he** needed help putting the phone down. He, with the help of a friend named Michael, created a simple and yet beautifully crafted wooden box with three instructions. Engraved on the inside of the box it says (1) Insert phone. (2) Close lid. Then, the lid of the box simply states (3) Be present. That's it. His message is simple and powerful. When you are distracted by your phone, you are not really present. If it takes having a small handmade box adorning your table to remind you to tune back in to others, then this box's worth is priceless. Mark Love's words share a story to which many of us can relate:

> We should better learn to put our phones away and be present in the moment.
>
> Please don't think for a minute that I'm good at being present just because I came up with the idea for this box. Quite the opposite. I thought of it precisely because I'm <u>not</u> good at it. When I'm with friends, if I'm not looking at my iPhone I'm thinking about looking at it. When I'm with my family, I'm the one with a hand holding the phone and the other held up to signal, 'Just a minute . . .'
>
> And I realize that life didn't used to be this way. Not for me, and not for all the people I see at restaurants and parties and plays, sitting with friends yet looking at their phones instead of each other.
>
> And I'm aware of a shift in myself, in my mind. From focused to frayed, from single minded to scattered, from present to remote. I'm aware of the feeling that wherever I am I seem to be focused somewhere else, wanting something else.
>
> And I'm pretty sure that's a good recipe for sadness, depression, relationship problems, and feelings of alienation.
>
> What can anyone do about this new addiction so many of us seem to have? When you feel you have the whole world and everyone you know in your pocket, it can be so difficult to just stay focused on where you actually are, on just a few people . . .

*I know that people don't need a box in order to put their phone away and be present wherever they are. But what we do need sometimes is a reminder of what's important. So The Be Present Box is functional art. It's a reminder, whether or not you ever actually put your phone inside it, that we all have choices. No matter what the new technology is currently nipping at the heels of our attention, we still have the power to choose the better things.* Reprinted with permission.

Love's blog speaks to the heart of the matter. Love explains that he just wanted to help others to be present with the people around them. It may take a box, like Love's, or an accountability partner, such as a parent or friend, or even a timer reminding us to turn off the phone and put it away. Whatever it takes for you, it is worth finding. There will always be something to lose time over in this life, but the "somethings" will never outweigh the "somebodies" of our lives.

> *Which of these might be helpful for your family (tech time-out, a box)? How does it make you feel that our "somethings" sometimes get more attention than our "someones"?*
>
> *Kid's reaction:* _____
>
> _____
>
> *Parents' reaction:* _____
>
> _____

Sheryl Cowling, a licensed clinical social worker who works in Christian family counseling, gives this advice:

*Balance is so very important to a healthy life that is pleasing to God. Balancing work and rest is necessary for wellness. If one spends too much time with electronics, an unhealthy balance will develop that can lead to problems emotionally, socially, academically, physically and even spiritually. It is wise to set limits on the amount of time one spends in front of a screen. It is wise to balance screen time with time spent worshipping God, enjoying nature, serving others, working to achieve personal goals, and enhancing relationships with family and friends. It is wise to balance passive time spent with electronics and active time spent enjoying other activities.*

Parents, can you see how balancing time on technology can be an opportunity to raise responsible and well-rounded children? Do you see opportunities to strengthen your relationship with your child as he or she sees you care enough to talk about these issues and that *you* trust him or her enough to take time and partner in this?!

Kids, do you understand that you can find balance in technology by using a phone responsibly and then putting the phone away to be present? Do you see the ability to love and honor God and your parents in this (and be blessed in many, many ways by this)?

*What is one of the blessings you think will come about as your family intentionally works to find this balance (time for family, an actual amount of time for fun on the phone, having your parents/kids see you as having valuable input)?*

Kid's response: _____

_____

_____

Parents' response: _____

_____

_____

He died for all, that those who live
should no longer live for themselves
but for him who died for them
and was raised again.
(2 Corinthians 5:15)

# Start the Communication— Reconnect

## Who are you?
### (Really—no cropping, posing, retaking, or editing your profile!)

*Note: This is a fun chapter of reconnecting (or maybe learning a lot that you didn't know about each other). Here are some options for completing this chapter:*

*1) Complete it like all the rest of the book— it'll go by quickly!*

*2) Use it for a rainy-day activity or your own weekend trivia game at home.*

*3) Break this chapter up and complete it in parts (but don't forget to come back and finish!).*

As children of God who want to become closer to each other and use technology in a balanced way, let's actually reconnect with each other. Kids, just because you've spent all your years with these people doesn't mean you know them as well as you think you do! Parents, the same is true! Look back, laugh, and learn about each other (and then dig deeper on your own!). There are no prizes to be gained; it's just a win-win as you strengthen your connection *and* reconnect (who knows, maybe later you'll break out the old home videos and board games you've forgotten about!).

*Parents and Kids:*
  *Parents (one or both):*

  *Where were you born?* _____

  _____

  _____

Who are your parents and original family unit?_____

_____

_____

Where did you grow up?_____

_____

What were some of the best things
about growing up where you did?_____

_____

_____

_____

Worst?_____

_____

_____

What did you want to grow up to be when you were a kid?

_____

_____

What did your career end up being and why?_____

_____

_____

_____

_____

Who were some of your best friends during your
childhood years?_____

_____

_____

_____

_____

What was a favorite part of your childhood?_____

_____

_____

_____

_____

What was one of the worst parts of your childhood?

_____

_____

_____

_____

What's something you wish you could change
from your childhood?_____

_____

_____

_____

_____

Is there anything you are thankful for now that you
didn't fully appreciate as a child?_____

_____

_____

_____

_____

What were the worst jobs/chores you ever had?_____

_____

_____

_____

_____

What was your favorite job in your
childhood/teenage years?_____

_____

_____

_____

What was your favorite book as a kid?_____

_____

What was your favorite game?_____

_____

What was your favorite movie?_____

_____

What was your favorite TV show?_____

_____

Who was your favorite teacher or another adult who
influenced you greatly?_____

_____

What was your favorite family trip, vacation,
or experience?_____

_____

_____

_____

_____

How did you spend your free time?_____

_____

_____

_____

_____

What do you miss being able to do or just generally miss
from those years?_____

_____

_____

_____

Kids:
What are some of the best things about growing up
where you live?_____

_____

_____

_____

_____

Worst?_____

_____

_____

_____

_____

When you were younger, what did you want to be when you grew up?_____

_____

_____

_____

_____

What do you want to be now?_____

_____

_____

_____

_____

Who are some of your best friends from over these childhood years?_____

_____

_____

_____

_____

What has been a favorite part of your childhood?_____

_____

_____

_____

_____

What has been one of the worst parts of your childhood?

_____

_____

_____

_____

What is something you wish you could change about your childhood?_____

_____

_____

_____

_____

Any regrets over things you wished you'd done
(or things you did do)?_____

_____

_____

_____

_____

Is there anything you are thankful for now that you didn't
fully appreciate when you were younger?_____

_____

_____

_____

_____

What have been the worst jobs/chores you've had?_____

_____

_____

_____

_____

What has been your favorite responsibility?_____

_____

_____

_____

_____

What was your favorite book as a younger child?_____

_____

What is your favorite book now?_____

_____

What was your favorite game as a younger child?_____

_____

_____

What is your favorite game now?_____

_____

_____

What is your favorite Bible story?_____

_____

_____

_____

_____

What is your favorite movie(s) or TV show(s)?_____

_____

_____

Who is a favorite teacher or an adult who has influenced
you greatly?_____

_____

_____

_____

_____

What has been your favorite family trip, vacation,
or experience?_____

_____

_____

_____

_____

How did you spend your time as a younger child?_____

_____

_____

_____

How do you spend your time now?_____

_____

_____

_____

How would you like to spend your time now?_____

_____

_____

_____

_____

*Parents:*

How do you like to spend your time now?_____

_____

_____

_____

_____

What is your favorite Bible story?_____

_____

_____

_____

What has been your favorite family trip, vacation, or
experience with your child?_____

_____

_____

_____

_____

What was one of the things that terrified you most about
becoming a parent?_____

_____

_____

_____

_____

What is something that you worried about before your
child(ren) was (were) born that was easier than you thought
it would be?_____

_____

_____

_____

What is something about becoming a parent
that you never realized would be so hard?_____

_____

_____

_____

_____

What are some of your greatest joys in being a family?

_____

_____

_____

_____

What have been some of the hardest parts of
being a family?_____

_____

_____

_____

_____

List two traits you saw early on in your child
(stories welcome 😊):_____

_____

_____

_____

_____

Share a struggle that was hard to watch your child
endure, but in the end it was for the best:_____

_____

_____

_____

_____

Share a laugh-out-loud episode of your child:_____

_____

_____

_____

_____

Share talents/traits that you've seen emerge and grow
in your child over the years:_____

_____

_____

Share one of your favorite things about your child:_____

_____

_____

What do you enjoy doing with your child?_____
_____

Share a moment in which you were proud of your child:_____
_____
_____

What would you love to do with your child if
time, money, and location were no issue?_____
_____
_____
_____

What are some things that you are thankful you are
able to give your child that you didn't have?_____
_____

What's something that you experienced or had as a child
that you wish you could give to your child?_____
_____
_____
_____
_____

Kids:
Relate a favorite story involving a parent:_____
_____
_____
_____
_____

Think through how one or both of your parents has taken
the time to be each of these roles in your life:
1) Teacher (taking the time to show or help you
   do something):_____
_____
_____
_____
_____

2) Coach (it doesn't just have to be sports, but how
   they gave advice to help you be the best you can be):

_____
_____
_____
_____

3) Defender (protecting you or showing how to
   stick up for yourself):_____

_____
_____
_____
_____

4) Biggest fan:_____

_____
_____
_____
_____

5) The Heavy (a time your parent disciplined you—
   although it hurt, you now see the benefit):_____

_____
_____
_____
_____

Any other special memories of your parent:_____

_____
_____
_____

### Kids and Parents:

Hopefully you saw new things in each other and things that remind you just how treasured and important you are to each other—gifts of God! Kids, did you see the love and remember more than just the person that is probably constantly tired and working hard every day? Parents, did you see that person you love dearly and remember why you work hard and still want to find time to play hard with him or her?

Parent reflection: "What do I want to intentionally pass on to my children (especially if I could ignore the pulls and pushes of daily life)?"

_____
_____
_____
_____

How am I doing on that?_____

_____

Kid reflection: Do I see my parents as real people who love me? How do I (or could I) take the time to show or say thank you for all they've done and do?

_____
_____
_____
_____

What were some things you didn't know about each other that you've just learned or realized?

Parents' response: _____

_____
_____
_____
_____
_____

Kid's response: _____

_____
_____
_____
_____
_____

Quick fact: "The average American sees 170,000 marketing messages by her 17th birthday" (Brown). Unless you decide to make the effort to keep learning about each other, spending time together, and growing together, you may find you know more *about the world and what it can offer* **than about the most important people in your life** (psst . . . these are the people God gave you, on purpose—people we want to value as gifts from God). And, although knowing how much spit/saliva you create in a lifetime is pretty cool, and knowing about or seeing all the popular movies in this decade is fun, it will never be as great as God's gifts to you in each other. *FYI, I've read that a person creates about two swimming pools full of spit/saliva in a lifetime* (Vecchione). But even more important than random facts is the fact that you can ask God to bless your relationships! He will bless you, and you can encourage each other to take time to talk and be together.

*List anything you saw in the other's response that gives you ideas of what you might want to do together (favorite movie marathon? trip out west? time to break out the photo albums?):*

*Parents' response:* _____

_____

_____

*Kid's response:* _____

_____

_____

Thank the Lord for his gift of families!

> Every good and perfect gift is from above,
> coming down from the Father
> of the heavenly lights.
> (James 1:17a)

# Regret and FOMO

Be very careful, then, how you live—
not as unwise, but as wise.
Ephesians 5:15

*Kids and Parents:*
*Forbes* magazine influences some of the wealthiest (and wanting-to-be-wealthiest) people in the world. Often, we are tempted to think those people would have fewer problems—they can just *buy* their problems away, right? It might surprise you, then, that *Forbes* magazine would direct these business titans to read and think about an article titled "The 25 Biggest Regrets in Life. What Are Yours?" The top regret in this article for hard-core money-makers was "working so much at the expense of family and friendships" (Jackson). Interestingly, ranking at 3 down the list of 25 was a regret of not getting off or away from the phone. These "have-it-all" people regret not spending time with their families and not being away from their phones more (not the opportunity to make even more money). Having a job is a good thing, and having a phone can be a good thing, but even good things can lead us away and distract us from more important things—like our connections to each other and God.

*Why do you think wealthy people regret not taking time away from their phones? Wouldn't more time on the phone equal more money?*

Parents' response: _____

_____

_____

Kid's response: _____

_____

_____

What things might these wealthy people value more than
more money (*hint, hint* and they'd put the phone away
for them):

Parents' response: _____

_____

_____

Kid's response: _____

_____

_____

Regret can often mean different things, like the word *love* can. We
can *love* those new jeans, we can *love* our pets, and we can *love*
that newest show on TV. Our feelings usually shape when and how
we use those words. There are differences in how deeply we love
things or people, despite how loosely we use the word. Regret is a
cousin to "love" in this sense. I can regret not going back to buy
those shoes because now they're gone, and now I'll have to pay
*so* much more to get them somewhere else! Or maybe we regret a
purchase that we felt pressured to make at the time. Had we slept
on it for a night rather than believe the salesman who said, "You'll
never get a deal like this! If you walk away, you'll pay more!" we
wouldn't have bought anything. Often adults will share that they
regret *not* having studied harder, *not* having tried studying for
a different degree or job, *not* having traveled more, *not* taken a
chance or opportunity, or just *not* having enjoyed just being a kid
when they were kids.

Kids, you've probably had regrets too. If only I hadn't lost it during
the game—that yellow card or foul could've been the difference
between winning and losing. If only I hadn't said that comment
about so-and-so—she really isn't that bad, but I just got caught
up in the moment. If only I'd not been so shy—maybe I could've

tried out for the part, the team, or asked out the person I've liked forever. If only . . .

As with degrees of love, the degrees of regret carry different weight too. The regret of not buying a pair of shoes on sale will carry on until a better deal, or something "that works," comes along (*don't get me wrong, some shoes will always touch a sweet memory—like the light up shoes when you were five?*). However, the regret of not buying new tires when recommended will probably carry a bigger weight, especially if you have a serious accident. That will probably reshape your thoughts on taking care of tires for the rest of your life (*a little more serious than the shoes regret*).

*Any little regrets you can think of (recently or in the past)?*

*Parents' response:* _____

_____

_____

_____

_____

_____

*Kid's response:* _____

_____

_____

_____

_____

_____

The same amount of time exists every day. We are in charge of how we use our time. As imperfect people, we will always doubt and second-guess certain decisions we've made in the past. We can't change those, but we can take steps to take charge of our future time together. We don't need to be helplessly dragged behind the clock, dragged through life. We have choices.

As a teacher, I often remind the students that none of us will be here in one hundred years (*and yes, there is usually one smarty-pants who has to question that*). That concept at first seems frightening—we are going to die—but after a moment of hard thought, most of my students realize the peace that comes from knowing there is an end to our time on this earth. We sometimes call our time on this earth our "time of grace." This is the time we are given to live here and to hear about Jesus—to hear the good news that Jesus is true God who came to earth and died for us. Remember that Bible passage from Chapter 2? "Faith comes from hearing the message, and the message is heard through the word about Christ" (Romans 10:17). We noted it then to see how amazing God is that he changes our hearts with his Word in the Bible. On our own we would be stubborn and self-centered, thinking we have all the answers, not actually knowing what matters. But God loves us so much that he didn't want to leave us like that! He wants us to know that we need Jesus because we needed a Savior. We needed him to die for us and then (yes!) rise from the dead so that we could go to heaven when our time here is up. TV and media show heaven in lots of ways, but the heaven the Bible promises will be without trouble, pain, or sin. It will be a place of true perfection. Now, because I'm so thankful that I get a great life of blessings now *and* a future life with God in heaven, I want to spend the rest of my days sharing that news with others and living in ways that show God I'm thankful for this gift of a Savior. When we talk about this, my students realize (at least for a part of a day) that there are things that matter more in life: family, friends, God, and the sure hope of heaven.

Also, they realize that there are things that *don't* compare and *aren't* worth chasing after. We can become soooo caught up in trying to have the newest game, phone, clothes, shoes, etc. that we lose focus on our main goals. Those other things are certainly gifts from God, but the people God has given to us are still more important and irreplaceable. We are challenged to find the balance we've talked about so that we don't regret not spending time with our family, especially parents, whom God has asked us to honor and promised to bless us when we do (remember that blessing of a long life from earlier?). And we especially want to share our Savior with others, showing through our lives (honoring parents, taking care of the things God's given me) that we love God.

43

Parents:

Do you have regrets from the past? Were there things you feel you wasted your time or money on that really didn't help you in the end?

_____

_____

_____

_____

_____

Regrets concerning your family?_____

_____

_____

_____

_____

_____

Kids:

What are some of your bigger regrets? Do you look back and wish you would have done or said things differently? Or that you had spent your time on different things?

_____

_____

_____

_____

_____

Any regrets concerning your family? Do you wish you hadn't gotten angry over a trip that you ended up enjoying, or was there some activity you wish you would've joined the family in instead of doing what you wanted at the time?

_____

_____

_____

_____

_____

# FOMO (sister to Regret)

*Kids mostly (Parents, tag along):*

Thinking about the walks down memory lane in the last chapter, it's probably safe to say that you do have good memories with your parents. You're probably not against having more memory-making experiences with them either. Then *why* does it seem so hard to balance the time you want to spend with your family (or know you might regret not having taken!) or with other things? Why is it so hard sometimes, especially since you do love them.

Is it possibly because of all the choices? Decisions, decisions! There's just *so* much out there to check in on and keep up with—and so little time.

FOMO—*"Find Out More Online"?* Nope. FOMO stands for "Fear of Missing Out." It may be new to you, but it's actually a word—a slang word, but still a word even listed in current dictionaries. The actual FOMO *sensation* has probably existed nearly as long as humans have. Adam and Eve were the first people God created. They worshiped God by taking care of the Garden of Eden, by walking and talking with him when he visited them there, and by *not* eating from the tree of the knowledge of good and evil. (Do you remember this story? It's in your Bible in Genesis chapters 2 and 3.) We could say that when Eve took fruit from this forbidden tree, she experienced FOMO. She *thought* she was missing out on something—unfortunately she was—it just wasn't the **good** her heavenly Father had in mind for her, and it would have deadly consequences. You see, after eating from the tree, she and Adam knew good **and evil**—seconds earlier, they had **only** known good. They had sinned against God, and their sin would eventually cause them to die—just like we too all die because we are sinful. Thank goodness Jesus took our place so that through faith in him we *only* die on earth, not forever in hell, separated from God (which would be eternal FOMO)!

Every person, since the very first people, has probably known someone who always wants (NEEDS) to be where something is going on. It may have been the child who always wanted to know, "What are we doing now, Mommy?" after the already long day *(and she wants to say, "*<u>Going crazy</u>*!" but doesn't* 🙂 ). It might be the teenager who is always jumping from activity to activity or circle of friends to circle of friends (and often burns out friends by "dropping" them for anyone else who *seems* more interesting at the time). For adults it may be less obvious, but it may show up as the person who needs to be everywhere that is "in," have all the right things, and just gives the illusion of being happy but never actually is.

Most adults would tell teens that whether they did or did not enjoy their junior high/high school/college days, they would *never* want to go back. Why is that? Why are most **content** not to relive those years?

*Parents: Comments on those years gone by? (And why you are thankful you can't relive or don't have to relive those years!):*

_____

_____

_____

_____

_____

Really, those years can be the best and worst years (and sometimes simultaneously the best and worst!). Those years are overrun by activities, groups, friends, and fitting in with different classes and groups of people (and then figuring where you fit *within* those different classes and groups). Those were busy years before cell phones. Now? It's nearly overwhelming how overly connected a person could be. It used to be that a person might stress over a tryout, a grade, an outfit—but Mom and Dad would calmly remind him or her that *there is nothing you can do by worrying about it, so go to bed and leave it until tomorrow.* The worrying part hasn't changed—you still can't change anything by worrying. Jesus lived through this world's stresses and busyness; he knows how we are tempted to worry! He even told us, "Do not worry, saying, 'What shall we eat?' or 'What shall we drink?' or 'What shall we wear?' . . . your heavenly Father knows [what] you need" (Matthew 6:31,32). What has changed is the lightning speed with which word (or any type of communication!) spreads. Today, the tryout that was embarrassing isn't just on view for those who saw it at the tryouts. Anyone could have pulled out a phone and recorded the whole experience, making it nearly viral before the person even leaves the tryout! Good news, bad news, blah-blah-ho-hum-news about the dog or lunch—it is all updated all the time! The result: an already crazy, busy time of life becomes more stressful. You now know what is going on and what is being buzzed about all over the place all at once (imagine your four friends holding your arms and legs and then pulling in different directions). FYI, before cell phones *(brace yourself for a SHOCK)* kids were *still* buying clothes, enjoying time with friends, being in sports, and experiencing emotions. But *now* it looks more like a tornado of "withmyfriendsatthemalldidn'tlikethatmoviegotahaircuthedoesn'treallylikehershefailedherbiologytestIcan'tbelievesheworethatdress." And it keeps going and going and going. It's kind of like a merry-go-round that can't stop. If you're not really busy or interested in what you are *supposed* to be doing *(which I'm sure never happens—especially during math homework or super-fun writing projects* 😊*)*, you could keep checking in *again* and *again* and *again*. So—*is checking my phone constantly really so bad?* Ask yourself this question:

## Am I Living nOW?

If you answered a text in the last 10 seconds, somebody out there *does* know you are alive. You are *technically* living. But are you living in the right now?

*Are you living now or in the past (posts/newsfeeds/videos)? Explain why you think you live now or in the past:*

*Kid's reaction:*_____

_____

_____

_____

*Parents' reaction:*_____

_____

_____

_____

Quick stat: "89% of 18-24-year-olds check their mobile phones within 15 minutes of waking" (Brown).

*Carpe diem*—it means "seize the day" in Latin. You might have heard the phrase in class (*parents may be purposefully forgetting this* 😊). The *carpe diem* poets wrote about living and living deeply because no one knows the length of his life. It is a very romantic, carefree idea. Who isn't inspired by thoughts of taking charge of the day, or life, and making memories? Truly, none of us knows how long we will live. (*Like, why am I going to school today—I might not live until tomorrow!* I don't really recommend trying that argument on Mom or Dad, but you get the idea!).

So back to the question: Are you living now??? Are you living, or just surfing to see what *everyone else did in the last 24 hours* (or possibly even less time since you were face-to-face)?

Is the new mantra (theme) of the times "carpe-the-last-24-hours"?

Are people today furiously watching and checking everyone else's lives go by without living their own lives? (FOMO over everyone else's lives?)

Will the 22-year-old **you** look back to your teen years and think, "Man, I wish I'd spent more time tweeting/messaging/texting?"

Is FOMO or boredom causing people to constantly check in on everyone else's life, with the sad result **that each person is only missing out on living his or her own life?**

*So are people missing out on their own lives to look at everyone else's lives? (Do you see people more interested in watching other's lives on their phones than what is in front of them?)*

*Kid's reaction:*_____
_____
_____
_____

*Parents' reaction:*_____
_____
_____

As we seek to control the ever-ticking clocks of our lives, let's prioritize what is truly important. After deciding what's important (family, God), let's try not just saying "I love you," but *showing* "I love you." Make it important so it does not become the regret of tomorrow. Regret that you ordered vanilla instead of chocolate, not that your phone was more important than being with your family.

We love
because he first loved us.
(1 John 4:19)

# Emily Post, and Why You Run Into People in the Mall

## (Separate Togetherness?)

### Part I

*Kids and Parents:*

Emily Post may well be turning over in her grave; you can hardly even go to the mall without running into people. Society is continually morphing and changing (or at least *recycling*) its standards. Do you ever look around—really look around and just "people watch"? What do you notice? In most any large gathering place, you will see people looking at their phones, talking, texting, and all while being in a large sea of people. (Maybe think of cattle milling around one another, but they have cell phones.) If you've never noticed this, stop and "people watch" for awhile—it's a scary and fascinating happening; it's a separate togetherness.

> *If you've noticed, where do you see people gathering on their cell phones and ignoring everyone around them in "separate togetherness" (feel free to comment on it too ☺)?*
>
> *Kid's reaction:*_____
> _____
> _____
> _____
> _____

*Parents' reaction:*_____

_____

_____

_____

Who is Emily Post? If you've never heard of her, she was the queen of etiquette (aka the "right way to do things") in the early 20th century. Whether you needed to know if you should write a thank-you note or how to excuse yourself (*you know, get out of something without making anyone mad* 😊), you simply checked what Emily Post said. And why is she rolling in her grave (*because she wants to join the zombie apocalypse at the mall?—hardly!*)? After thousands of years of regular social "rules," it looks like we've abandoned the "rules" with hardly a backward glance. For centuries people have been taught that a person should *look* at another person when talking to him or her. No matter how bored or *un*interested you were, you politely gave your attention to the other person/people with you. There were strict rules about what people could discuss. The weather was okay, but politics were a no-no. People made small talk and asked about each other's lives (however, don't get *too personal;* that's a no-no too). And, yes, you could argue that some of the conversations were just shallow because "good manners" limited people on what they could *actually* talk about. The point is this: **People took time to zero in on the people around them!** Again, you could argue that people weren't being **"real"** (authentic), but the point here is more about *value* (which was shown by society's rules). The value represented was this: I will give my attention to you because I see (I *value*) you as a person. *Just* because you are *near* me means that you are important enough to have my attention.

*Could you converse in a 20th-century parlor? Piece of cake, or would you stare at the cake? What's your reaction to this concept of paying attention to the people we talk to?*

*Kid's reaction:*_____

_____

*Parents' reaction:*_____

_____

Like the mall of "zombies," we're also sending messages every time we sit with other people and don't see them. What? We sit and watch what's trending, who's dating, who's celebrating, who's moping on social media, and what the funniest new video is. That's all usually fine—and often very fun! It also can send the message that someone else (or something else) is more important than the people actually around us. The basic truth is that **we're ignoring one another to see someone (or again, something) else.** It's the irony of the age—this separate togetherness. (Get it? We're together, but our activities make us as good as gone—*sayonara, adios.*) Some think that this shows incredible rudeness. Others take it as the new social normal—that people multitask (jumping from texting, to email, to internet videos, etc.) in front of one another, even to the exclusion of one another. Even the family room usually has a TV to captivate us instead of people needing to *actually communicate* for entertainment.

*So what do you honestly think? Are people who are physically <u>together</u> AND <u>using phones</u> at the same time being rude? Why or why not? (And does your view depend on if <u>you</u> are doing the multitasking versus someone else? Like, it's okay when my device works, but if it is dead and everyone else is ignoring me, it's not okay . . .)*

*Kid's reaction:*_____

_____

*Parents' reaction:*_____

_____

*Think about your family gatherings. Write down what your family is commonly doing when gathered together in a dining/living/family room:*

*Parents' viewpoint:*_____

_____

_____

*Kid's viewpoint:*_____

_____

_____

_____

When you are gathered, most likely you wrote that people are eating, someone is checking social media, someone may be reading, someone is watching TV, and/or someone is playing an onscreen game. Many of these are simply pastimes (things we do to "pass the time") and are **not** in any way wrong. The goal here is to analyze and look at *how* your family spends time when you are together.

*Think about what you wrote above. Is what you do when together <u>helping</u> or <u>hurting</u> your family's connectivity rating? (Do those activities draw you closer, or are you all loners, even though you are in the room together?)*

*Parents' truthful response:*_____

_____

_____

*Kid's truthful response:*_____

_____

_____

*Do you often make eye contact and actually know how the others are doing? Rate yourself 1–10 (1 being low, 10 being the best family connectedness ever—they could do a reality series on your awesomeness\*). Answer with your ideas, and know that Part II of this chapter will give you a few more ideas!*

*Parents' truthful response (and then what are your ideas for possibly helping this connectivity?): 1 2 3 4 5 6 7 8 9 10.*

_____

_____

*Kid's truthful response (and then any ideas for possibly helping this connectivity): 1 2 3 4 5 6 7 8 9 10.*

_____

_____

*If you are reality show-bound, you may use this space to name your new series._____

_____

_____

This technology is not going away. Emails will still need to be checked, text messages may need an immediate answer, and TV and social media allow many people different ways to unwind, laugh, keep in touch, or just learn.

Is there possibly a way to carve out time where the goal is to connect first—or even after some "downtime"/ "free time"?

Parents' thoughts/suggestions:_____

_____

_____

Kid's thoughts/suggestions:_____

_____

_____

The point: Be aware of the messages you are sending to others (and that's not just electronically ☺). When you give your attention to a device, even if there *are* people on the other side of the device, you may *appear* like a blinking sign that shouts to anyone else in the room, **"You're not really important to me—or at least not as important to me as whoever or whatever is on this screen."** (Just a disclaimer, you have to IMAGINE those words blinking <u>on your own</u>—feel free to reread them and imagine them blinking around you like a strobe light when you disconnect from others.) To recap, humans **need** human smiles, human eye contact, and human care (no offense to pets). *Intentionally* (that's on purpose) checking in with each other, even a *little,* can go so far in the seas of people (or cattle) drifting aimlessly around each other.

<u>So time for brutal honesty</u>—rip off the Band-Aid (kids will not be grounded, I hope, and parents need not return those "parent of the year" awards . . . yet). Have you ever felt like the screen mattered more than your parent or child, and when or why?

Kid's response: _____
_____
_____
_____

Parents' response: _____
_____
_____
_____

We want to understand that all people have value. (Especially remember that God valued us enough to save us and that parents and children have value in their God-given roles to train a child or to be a respectful child). If I gave you a 1-10 scale on whether you value each other, you would most likely respond with a 10. Unfortunately, our actions, as we talked about above, may be sending the opposite message.

## Part II: Solving Separate Togetherness
## Love = Value = Action

**Dear children, let us not love with words or speech but with actions and in truth.** 1 John 3:18

Please don't misunderstand! God does want us to love with words, but you've likely heard the expression that actions speak louder than words. Our actions show that we really do believe what we say we do! Again, love each other, say it, and then show it.

### Kids and Parents:

 No one needs to give up the phone, the games, the videos, or leave the room to hide so you can surf without feeling guilty. There are several options before hiding away (keep the phone, keep the games, stay together; think of it as having your cake and eating it too—*remember chocolate, not vanilla, though #noregrets #eatyourchocolatecake*). But think, how can you stay together and have fun (because you might be thinking this is some sort of punishment, like "together = + family and – phone")? Here are a few ideas:

**Assign times for those "tech time-outs"** (from Chapter 3).

**Share what you're looking at.** This may be awkward at first, but you can show each other what you've found and enjoyed online. Kids, your parents may not have the time to find all the funny videos you can, but they sure could use the laughs. Throw that funny video on the TV, or sit together and share what's trending or "who's doing what." You won't regret having the laugh together. Sit and look at media streams or sports highlights together—it may not seem like much at first, but the bonding will be a blessing for your relationship.

**Announce what you're doing.** Yes, actually tell everyone you are going to be looking at [whatever you are looking at], and offer that you are still available to the group. This may seem really odd, but it shows the people around you that they are important and that you are *available at any point* to communicate. If you are always looking down at a device, you may seem closed off from everyone or possibly not interested. Intentionally letting people know that you are available tells others that you do care and that you **would** and **do** want to interact with them (and it keeps you from wanting to find a reason to hide away in your room to do [whatever you are doing]).

**Plan together to find specific kinds of information from the internet or social media.** Many parents or family members don't have time to stay up on what's going on in the world *and* work and keep you alive. Decide that the kids (or one person a day) will share the top news stories, trending stories, or a few things going on in friends' and families' lives. Your own "top ten" could be better than any news or talk show, and it gives you the added bonus of sharing time together (media multitasking with a great purpose, yay!).

**(Kids) Text your parent.** You know your parents love you. Just like you want to hear from your friends, your parents want to hear from you too! Remember, they anticipated you, they planned for you, and they want to be part of your life. You honor and respect them by intentionally giving some of your time back to them. They rejoiced at your first words, first steps, first *anything* and *everything* (*well, okay, maybe not everything*). They even anticipated you needing to be able to take care of yourself and a household someday (yes, even thank them that they make you do chores!). But what they probably didn't anticipate, or want to even think about, was their own child *not* communicating with them. They don't need much, just send a "Thanks," "I love you," or a selfie (*remember, they're probably seeing the top of your head more these days, so they'd love to see your face* 😊 ). These little things show that you honor, respect, and value your parents ( 📖 *and* God promised to bless the families who live out love and respect—nice bonus!).

**Use internet resources as helps!** There are many techno-logical "helps" out there to help parents and kids curb the draw of being on devices and then find time for one another! Websites like ikeepsafe.org, netsmartz.org, teensafe.com, fosi.org, common-sensemedia.org (and many more!) give advice to parents to help find good technological boundaries—advice such as having devices charge out of the bedrooms or turning the devices off an hour before bedtime to encourage restful sleep.

*Which of these "helps" sound interesting to you? Why? (Or what might you add?)*

*Kid's reaction:*_____

_____

*Parents' reaction:*_____

_____


Do nothing out of selfish ambition or vain conceit.
Rather, in humility value others above yourselves,
not looking to your own interests
but each of you to the interests of the others.
(Philippians 2:3,4)

57

# Identity "Fraud," Fibs We (May) Allow Ourselves to Believe, and Grandma

*Kids mostly (Parents, tag along):*

## Identity or Identity "Fraud"— Who Are You, Anyway?

Parents don't want their kids to miss out on living their own lives (remember FOMO, the sister of regret?). Parents also don't want you to become mistaken about how life should look or miss out on the reality happening around you. In an article trying to help people overcome FOMO, an author warns that social media "doesn't provide a very well-rounded picture of people's lives. It's more like the cherry-picked perfection version" ("FOMO: This is the Best Way"). If you haven't noticed, just because people look a certain way in a picture doesn't mean that's what people look like all the time. Life is messy and uncomfortable at times, and usually it doesn't look like a commercial ad (in other words, perfect). People repeatedly check social media apps (FOMO, anyone?), and it can lead to problems. It's easy to start thinking that *everyone else has a better life*  just because it looks nice online, where people share the candy-coated, cropped, and posed versions of life.

> Is reality confusing because of posts and what we
> see online? In other words, are online things fake? Do we
> think everything is perfect because of what's online?
> Or is the "reality" we see online somewhere in the middle
> of fake and perfect?

Kid's reaction:_____

_____

_____

_____

_____

_____

Parents' reaction:_____

_____

_____

_____

_____

_____

Not *everyone* on social media paints this perfected version of life. Some people are very candid (or *real*) about the real happenings in life and even use social media to ask for help, advice, or prayers. But *many* use it to boost their self-esteem (whether they honestly realize it or not). How? Remember when you were a little kid and you got a sticker, or two or three of them, and it was enough to make your day? The number of "likes" (or "hearts," etc.) can become addictive (something you get and then want more and more and MORE of).

Have you seen people obsessed with how many likes/hearts they get? How do they act? (Posting ALL the time to get more, always posting crazier and crazier stuff?):

Kid's reaction:_____

_____

_____

Parents' reaction:_____

_____

_____

Unfortunately, for those "addicted," if you don't get that wanted attention, it could lead to becoming discontent, hurt, or even depressed. Having your confidence depend on other people's reactions is always going to be unsettling and nerve-wracking! *Will they like it? Will everyone ignore me? Will this get made fun of, or will it make me popular?* The unknown reaction of their friends often causes people to carefully write and pose for their pictures. The tug-of-war of wanting to be connected to others *and* wanting approval can cause people to become less authentic, or real. Sadly, a person may even unintentionally cause others to compare themselves to each picture or status and feel bad about their own lives. When you see another person that appears to have it so much "better" than you do (never mind that they only worked hard to make it *look* better), it may make you feel: *"I'm missing out on life because my life doesn't look like this."* It's possible that "by presenting your carefully edited version of life awesomeness, you just made anyone who sees it feel worse" ("FOMO: This is the Best Way"). Suddenly, it feels like "The Emperor's New Clothes," where everyone speaks carefully and no one wants to say the wrong thing—even if he or she knows better! Everyone is trying to show others the best, but it can really come off as shallow—however many "likes" there are.

*Do you see people "collecting ego stickers" (needing to be liked/acknowledged online to keep existing) or anxious about themselves because of how perfect or popular their friends seem to be on social media? How does it look?*

Kid's reaction:_____

_____

_____

_____

_____

_____

Parents' reaction:_____

_____

_____

_____

_____

_____

Food for thought (*mmmm . . . chocolate sprinkles?* 😊): Does posting have to be so nerve-wracking? Who are you trying to impress—the girl who sits behind you in science? Any guesses on who should *actually* be at the top of the list? Your parents! Yes, they may embarrass you from time to time (*feel free to write anything in the margin that you want to take up with them on the "you embarrass me" topic*), but, really, they are at the top. It's not just because they keep you alive and buy you stuff (*although, that's nice and you could thank them for that too*), but it's because God expects you to honor them. Remember that command and promise you highlighted in the value section: 📖 "Honor your father and your mother, as the LORD your God has commanded you, so that you may live long and that it may go well with you" (Deuteronomy 5:16). It may not seem so nerve-wracking if you remember that you *don't* have to impress all those people and you can instead focus on honoring your parents. For better or worse, your parents are the people you will be connected to always. It seems weird now, but you may not live near, see, or really know your current friends in ten years. Your parents will still be cheering you on, though—loving you whether you are in college, newly married, or a new parent in 10+ years (*and, yes, that thought might scare all of us* 😊).

> *Parents share: Do you keep in touch with anyone you knew when __you__ were your child's age? (And any tidbits of advice about how much life changes in a decade, from childhood to adulthood? If this feels heavy, add some sprinkles 😊).*

_____

_____

_____

_____

In addition to honoring parents because it's right and because they will actually be there for you as you continue to grow up, don't forget the promise that God will continue to bless you when you do this—"so that it may go well with you," he says. That's what *blessed* means: God puts something happy into your life, makes sure things go well. Again, who doesn't want to be blessed?! Who doesn't want God on their side, making things go well? Disclaimer: This doesn't necessarily mean you will have a mansion and unlimited resources (although you might!), but you will be blessed. It could be having a stable job, a great spouse, or amazing kids—just like you are, right!—or even just being happy and content (not something we always see in our world). *So, if I live showing that my parents are more important to me than all the likes and social media "friends," God promises that life will go well for me?* Well, actually . . . YES. He will be the one "carefully editing" your life and making it truly more awesome, not just awesome in a digital photo.

> *Could this happen? Could kids live for their parents' approval and happiness more than for the attention of their online friends? How so?*
>
> *Kid's reaction:*_____
>
> _____
>
> *Parents' reaction:*_____
>
> _____
>
> *What do you think of when you hear the promise "that it may go well with you"? Is this something that your family needs to talk about more? (How is your family doing well, or what can you improve to see the "it's going well" blessings?)*
>
> *Kid's reaction:*_____
>
> _____
>
> *Parents' reaction:*_____
>
> _____

Again, this fake-edited version of living is not true for all people on social media. Some people are genuinely just happy to see people they know and love and to see what they are doing in life. But, like most things, we humans have a way of messing up almost anything. The nice words for one person on social media become the hurt of *why can't I be quite like that?* (or why didn't I get the praise or comments he or she did?). And, sadly, as long as we have words and life, *someone* at *some time* will be hurt too.

Where do kids fit in this? All across the board.

One teen (name omitted for privacy), when asked about how real and authentic kids are on social media, said that kids will seek one another out on social media for fun, of course, but also when they are struggling. Some will share problems to a small group of trusted friends for help and encouragement. Thankfully, there are kids connecting to help and support one another—and not just to be on top of the social pyramid or get ego boosts.

*Kid's reaction: How do kids you know use social media? To feel better about themselves and look better than others? Or do you see people reaching out to one another to help? (if so, how?)*

_____

_____

_____

_____

*Parents' reaction: What negatives and positives do you see for your child and his or her friends in all of this? (Are there parts of this social media system you like—pun intended—or don't like for the kids?)*

_____

_____

_____

_____

Kids (and parents!) are seeing huge differences in how other kids present themselves. Is a picture always carefully posed? No. In fact, some kids love using social media to send ridiculous and "ugly" (purposefully being silly, etc.) pictures to each other for fun. Some collections made for other kids are of all the funny/silly/ridiculous pictures they've gathered of each other just for fun. It is pretty hilarious *and* a little refreshing compared to the carefully posed "perfect" pictures.

## Fibs We (May) Allow Ourselves to Believe

On another side of this, though, are not just the pictures that are carefully posed to show the best light, angle, or smile. Unfortunately, we live in a culture that is weighed down with pictures, movies, ads, etc., of people appearing more as objects than as people! (This is objectifying: seeing people only for how nice they look instead of remembering and caring about them as people.) According to the American Psychological Association (APA), the "objectifying" does affect females and males, but stats show it's extremely lopsided—especially toward female objectification (Zurbriggen et al.). These images may cause girls to feel pressured into looking a certain way. As if there weren't enough pressures just finding out "who you are," now the pressures to look and dress "right" (again, how the media says you should dress) are just more added pressures online *and* in person.

In what ways have you noticed that toys, ads, or movies show "how we should look" in ways that may not be realistic or helpful?

Kid's reaction:_____

_____

_____

_____

_____

_____

Parents' reaction:_____

_____

_____

_____

_____

_____

The American Psychological Association addressed the issue of objectifying with a 44-page report that warns how seeing these warped pictures of how a female "should look" limits a young female's ideas of how she should or can look "by putting appearance and physical attractiveness at the center of women's value" (Zurbriggen et al.). Again and again, the study pointed to examples which have directly or indirectly shown girls that they need to achieve a certain level of "perfection" to be loved and accepted in society. That is an impossible standard! Perfection was lost way back in the Garden of Eden (remember Adam and Eve's *actual* perfect paradise). The person he or she is, whom God created, is 📖 "fearfully and wonderfully made" (Psalm 139:14), despite society's standards for weight, height, hair color, etc. The devil can work to wear away our confidence through these unreal standards of society. It is not how you look, what you wear, or who you hang out with but knowing you are loved by God and your family that gives you confidence. You may be made fun of for not changing to please others in what or how you update posts and responses. God and your family (*okay, maybe not your big brother*) will always, without hesitation, "like"—even more strongly, *love*—you, despite what the number of responses may show under a picture or post. No matter the hateful, awful, or jealous words thrown at you for not following the crowd—or, perhaps even more scary, the *silence* of no response from others—we take our comfort and confidence in this: 📖 "Neither death nor life, neither angels nor demons, neither the present nor the future, nor any powers, neither height nor depth, nor anything else in all creation, will be able to separate us from the love of God that is in Christ Jesus our Lord" (Romans 8:38,39). Neither society nor following the trends nor mean "friends" nor unreasonable standards can separate us from the love of our Savior (and the family he gave you!). Rejoice for that and enjoy! And don't let the "likes" (or lack of them) change your standards!

*Kid's reaction: What are some of the current ideas for how you should look, wear your hair, and dress?*

_____

_____

_____

*Do any of those current ideas really bug you? Or maybe you wish you could follow them, but you can't afford them, can't make your hair do that, or will never physically be able to do that or look like that:*

_____

_____

_____

Have you noticed any examples on media or TV of people being objectified—the focus is more about what he or she looks like? Please share (like using a woman's blowing hair and heavy make-up to help sell computers?—yes, ridiculous!)

Kid's reaction:_____

_____

Parents' reaction:_____

_____


Honestly, you may not always appreciate the body God's given you just because of these objectifying pictures. Have you ever thought less of yourself after comparing yourself to these images? How or why?

Kid's reaction:_____

_____

Parents' reaction:_____

_____


In the Bible, King David described how amazingly God created you, saying in Psalm 139:14, 📖 "I am fearfully and wonderfully made."

How does it feel to know the one who hung the stars in the sky thinks you are "wonderfully made"—awesome, even?

Kid's reaction:_____

_____


Kids: You not only have confidence if you have to go against what's popular (knowing God thinks you're pretty awesome—enough to die for you!), but God has also given you parents who think you are pretty awesome too. Remember, your parents are great resources to talk to in this! They may not care as much about what's "in" as you do, but they did face the same issues at your age, and they love you! In fact, in a study about teens and cell phones, 📱 the kids surveyed said that their parents have the *biggest* influence on what they will decide is appropriate or inappropriate behavior online (Lenhart et al.). (Just in case you thought none of the other kids are asking their moms or dads.)

*Parents' reaction: Do you remember those hard years? Or do you maybe still feel the pressure of fitting in to the world's standards? You also are "fearfully and wonderfully made." It may be challenging, but think of ways you can show your confidence (which doesn't bow to society's fads) in words and actions (and feel free to share experiences from those years!).*

_____

_____

_____

_____

Parents:

Think about how you listen to your child as he or she faces the pressures all around. Ask yourself, "Do I let her or him know I will listen without belittling the problem?"

*How can I make myself available as a good listener, a guide and sounding board, and someone who reflects the love and confidence I have for the Lord?*

_____

_____

_____

*Kids: How can your parents be there so that it's easier for you to go to them?_____*

_____

_____

Kids:

*This is a great chance to level with your parents if there's anything about yourself—"identity," your feelings, or, well, anything social media or otherwise—you've wanted to talk about but thought Mom or Dad wouldn't understand (this might be a great time to give them a chance to love and help you!).*

_____

_____

_____

# The Grandma Rule

Before you give up showering, changing your clothes, and washing your hair, know that your personal image does matter. Your "look" can be silly, and it can be fun. A good rule of thumb for posting any words or pictures is always "The Grandma Rule." If you would be embarrassed to have your Grandma see what you posted, you probably shouldn't post it. Really. Grandma is someone who loves you for who you are—a great reminder for you to stay true to your identity and NOT bend to the fibs that society is trying to convince you of.

And even more so, your love and thanks for God and what he has done is *actually* the best standard (*but having a picture of Grandma as your screensaver can't hurt as a reminder* 😊). The apostle Paul urges us on: "Whether you eat or drink or whatever you do, do it all for the glory of God" (1 Corinthians 10:31). Paul is saying that our eating and drinking could honor God. Interesting? Maybe you've never thought about your everyday actions as honoring or not honoring God. When I take care of my body by eating and drinking healthy things *because* I love and respect the body God's given me, I can honor God. I can decide to eat the right amount of food (*maybe not eating the whole carton of ice cream . . . for several reasons* 😊) as a thank-you to God. I can work to my ability on my schoolwork (and that may be A, B, or C work—but it is the best *I* can do) as a thank-you to God for my abilities. I can be patient with my family or friends, or I can be kind when it would be so much easier to be sarcastic as a thank-you to God for how patient he is with me. I can thank God for my abilities by choosing to play sports fair, working hard, and going for the ball—not taking the cheap shots on other players.

So something as simple as commenting on a post takes a different view when I see it as something that *can* be done in a way to honor God, my family, and my good name (*and maybe throw Grandma in there too* 😊). I may stop and think, "Hmmm . . . what I first wanted to comment was funny, but it didn't really help my friend; it only made fun of him, and that doesn't show me as a good friend or a child of God . . ." And, if you have to even ask, "Is this crossing the line—going too far?" then you may need to go back to the reason you want others to see such a picture or post. If your reasoning again is for shock or to cut others down, then reconsider or reword your post. As Christians, we can see everything we do as an opportunity to reflect love for God. **The question then becomes, "How can I keep growing closer to my Lord? Will this picture/ post harm my relationships or pull me farther from God, or will it glorify my God in thanks for all he's done, draw me closer to others, and build them up?"** We have soooo much freedom, bought by our Savior, and now we have sooooo much opportunity to use it in thanks and praise to God!

Grandma Rule:

Kid's reaction: Are you going to put Grandma as your screensaver? Kidding aside (because you really could do that if you want), where do you see chances in your life to do things to God's glory (or places you already were, and never thought about those situations giving glory to God!)?

_____

_____

_____

_____

Parents' reaction: Where do you see areas in you and your family's life where you can say thank you to God (for instance, we're cleaning today as a thank-you that God gave us this beautiful house)?

_____

_____

_____

_____

Why does it even matter if what I post honors God?

Kid's reaction:_____

_____

_____

Parents' reaction:_____

_____

Quick stat: 👤📋 "64% of teens admitted blocking parents or family from a post or a friend request" (Brown). This stat shows that many teens are posting things that either they feel might be considered inappropriate by family OR they might not realize how this media could instead draw them closer to their families. This could be one more thing for many to regret later—*I didn't use this as another way to draw closer to the people who I know love me in the time I have with them.*

*Think about your <u>identity</u>, NOT bowing to society, and being loved while loving your family and Savior—what do you think about blocking family members from seeing your identity online (the quick stat above)?*

*Kid's reaction:*_____
_____

*Parents' reaction:*_____
_____

Quick stat: 👤📋 "55% of all online teens have decided not to post content that might reflect poorly on them in the future" (Lenhart et al.).

Unpost? Yes, words can be deleted or removed from a post—but they can't be fully removed (from "memories," or screenshots, etc.). And although pictures can be pulled down or disappear, as some apps are designed to do, they can never fully be *unseen*. Just like something you shouldn't have said or didn't want to see, you can't fully erase it from your memory. And digitally, there's an even longer memory. A picture that you posted—ho-hum, spur-of-the moment, or possibly in anger—**will always exist somewhere**. *You* may never be able to find it again, but your boss 15 years from now may be able to find it. And although you might not be looking for jobs now, your posts will follow you. 👤📋 "93% of hiring managers will review a social profile before making a hiring decision" (Davidson). Again, we want to have posts that honor our families' good names and put God first, but maybe you didn't realize that the mean posts from a sixth grader to another sixth grader could follow that student when she applies to jobs or colleges. It's certainly something to make you think. In 2017, Harvard University withdrew admissions from ten would-be students. Reason? Vulgar, thoughtless, hurtful memes—cartoons, video clips—they had shared in a private group chat (Natanson). Unfortunately, a site set up for people to get to know their future classmates spiraled into a private group so they could be edgier, funnier, and private—not any longer! Did you catch that? They shared in a *private* group, and now they are not going to Harvard. Only 6 of every 100 who apply to Harvard are actually admitted (PrepScholar). Imagine getting into your dream school only to lose it because of poor online choices.

*Have you seen anyone lose privileges (lose a phone, get grounded, etc.) because of poor social media choices? If not, do you or your friends know what the actual consequences would be if you were caught making poor online choices? ("Mom's going to kill me" doesn't count* 😃 *.)*

Kid's reaction:_____

_____

_____

_____

_____

_____

Parents' reaction:_____

_____

_____

_____

_____

While we're thinking about how the present affects the future, "66% of hiring managers said they would hold poor spelling and grammar against candidates" (Davidson). Today affects tomorrow—choices, choices. Friends can offer forgiveness, and God definitely offers forgiveness, but the *consequences* may still follow poor choices. I asked some fifth- and sixth-grade students what they thought about these stats—the fact that writing LOL,

IKR, GTG, HHSF and misspelling words could possibly cause someone *not* to hire you—and they were shocked.

> The Bible says, "The mouths of fools are their undoing, and their lips are a snare to their very lives" (Proverbs 18:7). What are your reactions to the possible damaging effects of posts, remarks, and poor spelling?
>
> Kid's reaction:_____
> _____
> _____
> _____
> _____
>
> Parents' reaction:_____
> _____
> _____
> _____

(And . . . *just in case any dinosaurs are reading this and need translation,* it was Laugh Out Loud; I Know, Right?; Got To Go; and Ha Ha So Funny).

Taking the time to think before posting can not only save you and others from hurt later on, but it can also be an opportunity to praise God and honor Mom and Dad (*who <u>will</u> need you to get a job one day and move out—that's sure to be a blessing for both of you!) Thinking* about your responses may not be as exciting as sending off a spontaneous comment, but it may serve you in the present and future and serve God and others right *now*.

> Can't "unsee" it, so don't post it: Have you seen this as a problem among your friends—what they post (or if you aren't on the same social media apps, have you seen and heard the problems it has cost others)? What's your opinion on the posts around you?
>
> Kid's reaction:_____
> _____
> _____
> _____

*Parents' reaction:*_____

_____

_____

_____

This chapter was all about being the actual you *(that's Y-O-U, in case you've been texting "U" and . . . um . . . got a little confused* 😊 *)*. YOU are still you—hopefully—and not trying to be someone else just because some people can't seem to actually own up to what they look like in real life (candy-coated identity fraud). You don't need to look like a commercial for shampoo when you post pictures *(but please continue to shower)*. And you have tools to help you think, like thinking of 👶 Grandma's response to seeing your text/post (and remembering that your words can honor your parents and God—and give you blessings in the future!).

*What is more helpful for helping you post/text responsibly (circle one):*

| Identity (You are you! Be that— but not "U!") | Stats of future employers not hiring . . . | Grandma Rule |
|---|---|---|

*Explain:*

*Kid's reaction:*_____

_____

_____

Be *you*—not "U."

> Seek first his kingdom
> and his righteousness,
> and all these things
> will be given to you as well.
> Therefore do not worry about tomorrow.
> (Matthew 6:33,34)

# Is There an Upside?

*Parents (Kids, ride along):*

In an article titled "I Thought Snapchat Was Ruining My Teen—But When She Landed in the ER, the Truth Came Out," Candice Curry shares the challenges of parenting children with the technologies of today. She admits that it freaks her out a little when her daughter takes 75 selfies on a three-minute ride to church (*it needs to be the right one, right?*). Kids may seem to take and send an excessive number of pictures of themselves (*makes those years of taking all those baby pictures seem tame!*). Curry goes on to recount how her daughter got very sick (yet continued to take and send pictures). What Curry saw then was a network of friends coming forward to help her daughter, through her daughter's social media community. Her daughter received love and gifts at her doorstep (face-to-face communication born out of social networking—huh?). Curry gives kudos to the kids of today: "We don't give this generation enough credit. . . . Their lives are being played out through social media in real-time right in front of all of our faces . . . but they're actually doing a pretty good job at making it work for them" (Curry).

*Are we giving kids enough credit that they are making good choices with time management and cell phone use? How?*

*Kid's reaction:*_____

_____

_____

_____

_____

74

*Parents' reaction:*_____

_____

_____

_____

_____

*What would you and your friends do (or have you done) to help one another—like the daughter and her friends?*

*Kid's reaction:*_____

_____

_____

*Parents' reaction (you may help your friends through social media, but if you aren't "there" yet, share a time you helped a friend):*_____

_____

_____

_____

*Parents, especially (Kids too):*

Once again, teaching a responsible balance of technology has no one-size-fits-all answer. As the Curry story shows, parents may "see" one side that could appear really shallow at times—selfie, selfie, selfie. However, the reality was that these children were not only socializing for fun, but they were also taking care of one another. The choices we make concerning rules for our children should not be aimed to impress or please our children, or other adults for that matter. Communication between kids and parents can help each side understand the other, before calling kids "shallow" or parents "dictators," while defining boundaries (wow!—see the upside!). We tinker and tweak and try what works in order to raise responsible children. We will fail at times (either by our own standards or the kids'). Tinker, tweak, and try again, focusing on the responsible Christian children you are helping to mold.

Think of a potter's wheel, if you will. The clay is shapeable, able to be formed and changed as long as it is still wet. Children are very similar—even teenagers are still forming and growing into the people they will become (hence, the *"formative"* years). You will make decisions about what your child may or may not have. It may seem like some decisions cause dings that make the whole piece of moving clay become a misshapen blob. So you add a little reinforcement (love, care, and time with them—much like wetting and smoothing the clay again), and you can work again to begin reforming this beautiful creation of God. The forming is a process— it could be longer and harder for some. It's okay to be conservative at your house, and it's also okay to trust your child with a little more freedom. As a parent, you are the one to help smooth out whatever bumps come up—children do need the guidance to become the Christian adults God has entrusted you to help form.

God has promised to be there in all times and all situations—and when you're not sleeping because of something that's gone haywire, remember that the Maker of the universe is already up and ready to listen, help, and equip you: 📖 "He will not let your foot slip—he who watches you will not slumber. The LORD watches over you—the LORD is your shade at your right hand" (Psalm 121:5). And how can he equip you? 📖 "Do not be anxious about anything, but in every situation, by prayer and petition, with thanksgiving, present your requests to God" (Philippians 4:6). Pray. Go to God's Word (like the kids, you can find these passages in your own Bibles to read and reread for strength, comfort, and support!): 📖 "All Scripture is God-breathed and is useful for teaching, rebuking, correcting and training in righteousness, so that the servant of God may be thoroughly equipped for every good work" (2 Timothy 3:16,17). God's Word offers direction for training these children—even on the days it feels like you're doing more rebuking or correcting than anything else!

*Parents' reaction: Think back to something you deliberately changed in your parenting because you didn't like it as a child (that "ding"—or at least what you perceived as a "ding"—while you were the forming clay).*

_____

_____

_____

_____

*Parents' reaction:* Think of something (rule, etc.) you didn't like having enforced on you as a kid, but now, as a parent, you can better appreciate it 🍩 (and maybe how you can encourage your child through this adult perspective toward rules, etc!).

_____

_____

_____

_____

*Kid's reaction:* Share some rule or guideline that you aren't terribly fond of right now (also why you think it should change and how it should change).

_____

_____

_____

_____

_____

*Parents' reaction:*_____

_____

_____

_____

_____

Communicate ➔ to understand ➔ and draw closer ➔ = upside 😊

## More Upsides

One benefit of living in the 21st century is that most people have enough food to eat. A downside of this is that many people have more food than exercise time, which often equals health challenges. One of the neat upsides of technology is all the activity trackers to encourage people to get out and move, monitor heart rate, and track distances run/walked. This has become not only a fun encourager to move and take care of bodies but a cross-generational, fun "competition" in my family. Truth be told, when competing for the most steps, usually my daughter beats her principal, dad, and grandma—but not always!

*Would you like to have (or do you have) a fitness tracker? What would be the fun of it? Or who would you compete with?*

*Kid's response:* _____

_____

_____

*Parents' response:* _____

_____

_____

There are even online programs to help you go from only walking to running a marathon. The teens I know often stream workout videos or just find workout tips online. They also look up recipes for smoothies *or* cookies (*they are real kids* 😊). Often we look up symptoms—do I have a cold or influenza? During an afterschool soccer game, I sat with Chris, our substitute goalie. He was only supposed to give our goalie a two-minute break. Unfortunately, another player headed Chris' arm instead of heading the ball in that short amount of time. We iced and looked up the symptoms of a break vs. sprain, texted his mom, *called* his mom, and looked up the urgent care we could meet at on the way back to school. The downside was that Chris was out of the season after less than two minutes of playing sub; the upside was he got care for a broken arm much more quickly thanks to technology!

*What kinds of healthy things might you look up online?*

*Kid's response:* _____

_____

_____

_____

*Parents' response:* _____

_____

_____

How about education? No groans! Really, just stay tuned. There are many educational sites that encourage learning—for free—and give rewards. The school where I teach encourages kids to keep working on math during the summer. Boring? It doesn't have to be— it has points that unlock prizes *(if you're into that)*, and it helps kids have confidence going into the next year. (I've even known kids to finish math courses ahead of grade level online—getting ahead for high school and college and saving the $$$.) Maybe math doesn't interest you as much, but the number of things you can learn by reading or watching videos is amazing. I spend hours in the course of a year watching videos to show in class, making science and social studies more interesting. It may take a while to find the perfect ones, but *I* learn a lot, and the kids love the visual learning! Also, my online library system is amazing—we can (and yes, we do—my whole family) borrow books or movies to phones or devices. One of my past students *(he'd say he's not a reader . . . but . . .)* finished the novel we were reading in class and *had* to have the next book (and then the third) to read. His mother bought it for him on his phone (she was so happy he wanted to read), and he was even allowed to read on it at school (it was reading—not social media ☺).

*What have you done online (or maybe will look up now) that's educational (or semi-educational ☺)?*

*Kid's reaction:*_____

_____

_____

_____

*Parents' reaction:*_____

_____

_____

_____

Honestly, I'm *always* looking up something. There truly is such an upside to having this technology so handy. I've found cleaning tips, recipes, ages of celebs, why a marathon is 26.2 miles, or how that one word I always seem to misspell is *really* spelled. (I have a friend whose cousin is from England—she didn't know this cousin even existed. She found her through online resources and social media! What a find!)

*What are some things you've looked up and learned recently (and if you're a parent, maybe* <u>*relearned*</u>*)?*

Kid's response: _____

_____

_____

Parents' response: _____

_____

_____

And . . . how *did* we live before online ordering and shipping (*I think fine, but* <u>*really*</u>*?*). I have family all across the country, plus a busy life. How awesome is online shopping, free shipping, and two-day shipping? The upside of *convenience* is priceless.

*Are there any online conveniences you love? (I broke my phone case—and replaced it online within two days).*

Kid's response: _____

_____

_____

Parents' response: _____

_____

_____

Sharing what you care about? I regularly post pictures from school life to our school social media page and web page. People love seeing what the students are doing—seeing love in action. And since I work at a Christian school, it also becomes one more way to share the love of Jesus with the community and, really, the world—since media can reach to nearly all corners of the world. (Want a way to share or learn about Jesus online? Check out and share www.whataboutjesus.com to learn about Jesus from home too—what an upside!) Many people use social media to check in on friends and family and to find out how they can pray for one another. Some want to be aware of what disasters or charities need relief.

There are truly so many upsides from this digital world: it is easy to care for one another, reach out to others, and learn about and take care of *nearly anything* we have in life!

In what ways can you show love and concern for others (friends, family, the world) online? How might you be able to share your love of Jesus (UPSIDE!)?

Kid's response: _____

_____

_____

Parents' response: _____

_____

_____

Love one another. As I have loved you,
so you must love one another.
By this everyone will know
that you are my disciples,
if you love one another.
(John 13:34,35)

# Yesterday, Today, and Tomorrow

*Parents and Kids*:

The earth turns, as expected, every day. Life is constantly happening around us. There are days when we'd all like to freeze time and let the moment last a little longer (and days we wish we could fast-forward through). Change happens constantly, even when we can't (or maybe *don't*) slow down long enough to notice—it's like one of those fast-motion documentaries where you see life pass by in a rainforest. You may think that nothing is changing, but when you watch the still camera fast-forward through a month, two months, or a year focused on one area of the forest, you see the flowers blooming, the insects morphing, and the trees really changing. Or maybe it's like when your aunt visits and gushes over how different you suddenly seem to look. You feel like everything about you is the same, but she sees the changes in you that you, well, can't even see when you're literally staring into the mirror at your own face every day!

You change, the way you do things changes, and what you  want will change. The same will be true for all your life, and that includes your digital life. Updates, new phones, new uses, or just what you do with your time on a phone will likely change (although, I do see an awful lot of adults playing the same games as kids—only time will tell what stays popular!).

Change *is* happening, but it also seems like we are constantly looking forward. We make goals, prepare, and plan for events in the future. We might have plans like needing to buy items for the upcoming sport, dance, or just dinners for the week. So let's look backward for a minute. One of my daughters and I were laughingly remembering a phase she went through when she was little. She now thinks it's hilarious that she ever thought it would be a good idea (stylish, even) to wear leggings under her shorts. I've assured her that she wasn't alone in this phase—other people had most definitely been wearing the same outfit in the same time period! Most people love looking back at pictures, yet it usually brings the same response: we end up laughing at some hairstyle or outfit. It's great fun, to be sure. It's also an *odd* part of being human. Why is it that we find something perfectly acceptable (*or, let's be honest, AWESOME*) at one point, and then later in time find it hilarious and/or embarrassing?

*Share a past phase you went through (or two, or . . . ) and your reaction to those phases now!*

*Kid: I remember when . . .* _____

_____

_____

_____

_____

_____

*Parents: I remember when . . .*
*(either about yourself, child, or both!)* _____

_____

_____

_____

_____

_____

Why does it happen that we are constantly changing looks, ideas, and styles? There are so many reasons for these phases. Sometimes changes happen because of boredom or just a *need* to change something—the ever-driving desire for *more* (or at least "different"). These *needs* are often led by the retail economy (commercials, ads, pop-ups), which is *always* changing, and even improving, the things of our lives (necessary AND unnecessary *things*). And we *have* to have them then, right? At least that's what they want us to believe.

Think about some fads from the past. For instance, I remember Christmas seasons when the big item was Cabbage Patch Kids, and years later it was Tickle Me Elmo. People stood in line and paid outrageous prices for something they thought their kids just *needed* to have.

List some items you remember being the BIG ITEM to have:

Kid's response: _____

_____

_____

Parents' response: _____

_____

_____

Think of anything right now that people currently NEED (or really, really want):

Kid's response: _____

_____

_____

Parents' response: _____

_____

_____

Free gift? Can anything "free" be good? I have lots of things that were free—but usually they are secondhand: furniture someone else is done with, clothes "handed down." *I* like those things, but not everyone likes used things. My sister once won a brand-new gaming console—most people would consider that better. Our greatest gift, Jesus, is free. He doesn't *change*. He bought us heaven (which is way better than being punished with the devil for all the bad and wrong we have done). He paid for it with his perfect life and death. Hmm . . . so now we have the best gifts for free—forgiveness, Jesus, heaven. No corporation is going to improve on any of those gifts—EVER. And God has blessed us with parents to love and raise us. In fact, everything else is a gift from him too. We really own nothing when you think about it: 📖 "The earth is the Lᴏʀᴅ's, and everything in it, the world, and all who live in it" (Psalm 24:1). The God who made everything with only his words and almighty power truly owns everything. 📖 "We brought nothing into the world, and we can take nothing out of it" (1 Timothy 6:7).

*Let's visualize how good we have it*:

| Me | Parents | God |
|---|---|---|
| *constantly* changing | | never changing |
| Wants: | Wants: | Wants:<br>✓ Us in heaven<br>(he gave us the free gift to get there)<br>✓ Our love and respect<br>(and love and respect toward the parents and possessions he gave us) |
| Needs: | Needs: | Needs:<br>✓ Nothing |
| Owns: Really, nothing<br>(but list some of the things God's given you): | | Owns:<br>✓ *Everything*<br>(including your cell phone, your clothes, your stuff . . .) |

Do we really realize how blessed we are? Do we pause and see everything we have belonging to God? It does. *Because* everything belongs to God, we are then managers of God's things (no matter what it is or how long you have it). You will never stop being a manager, even as you become older.

*List below what you are managing in "yesterday, today, and tomorrow" (and yes, you can have some fun answering or imagining the future things you'll manage 😊):*

| "Managing Age" | What I manage (kid) | What I manage (parent) |
|---|---|---|
| infant: | (ex: pacifier . . .) | |
| little child: | | |
| elementary school: | | |
| middle school: | | |
| young adult: | | |
| middle-aged adult: | | |
| senior citizen: | | |

God perfectly knows what we *need*, even if he doesn't always give us what we *want*. He knows us well and reminds us, "Keep your lives free from the love of money and be content with what you have, because God has said, 'Never will I leave you; never will I forsake you'" (Hebrews 13:5). The balance between a desire to "keep up with the Joneses" and being a contented, good manager of our things (or, really, God's things) will always be a challenge on this side of heaven. All the pop-up ads—what are they tempting you to buy lately? It's too bad there aren't ads that tell you how good you have it. Look around your room, house, school, and earth—all are God's. Have you thanked God today for the little and big things? Our culture makes it easy to be unthankful and discontent. It's a good thing that God leaves us encouragement (like the previous passage), promises to give all that we need, and blesses us beyond compare with family and friends to support us!

*Please share something that you "had to have" (whether you actually got it or not) because it was the newest thing:*

Kid:_____

_____

_____

Parents (yourself, your child, or both!):_____

_____

_____

Looking back, the things you "had to have" may be funny to think about again—just like those grade school or middle school hairdos that won't be repeated anytime soon. Another reason that we change (or "try on" change) is that we are trying to find out who we really are. This is not suggesting that you have an identity crisis, but truly using your gifts, discovering your gifts and talents, and "trying on" who you want to be—or will be—is a process that sometimes takes years (and may keep changing through the decades to come).

Part of the reason you need to discover who you are—and this is just the facts, not a judgment—is that our brains are still forming until the early 20s (National Institute of Mental Health). Teens from any time, past or present, are at an interesting time in development: they are really in the prime of life for physical health, strength, and mental ability (think of how much faster you can react or memorize than your parents). Those are great advantages, and they really show why many older people will sigh that "youth is wasted on the young." Those bonuses of being so lively contrast with the ⬛ statistic that *death* by injury jumps to *six* times higher for 15- to 19-year-olds than it is for 10- to 14-year-olds. Not only that, but the National Institute of Mental Health adds that crime for males in those years is at the highest rate and alcohol abuse is very high. (These behaviors can be partly caused by genes, past experiences, and environment too.) Studies of the developing brain show that basic functions mature first, but "the parts of the brain responsible for more 'top-down' control, controlling impulses, and planning ahead—the hallmarks of adult behavior—are among the last to mature" (National Institute of Mental Health). Huh??? It means that the cautious side of teen brains may take a vacation until around age 20. The emotional responses of teens are also more active than those of an adult, and yet "the parts of the brain involved in keeping emotional, impulsive responses in check are still reaching maturity" (National Institute of Mental Health). And **that?** It means that when—as a teenager—you feel a sea of emotions, you are perfectly normal (tears, uncertainty, etc.). It also means that teens may feel less restraint to do activities that are risky or off-the-wall than they would have when they were younger—and than they will as an adult. That can make spirit days at school very funny and being silly with your friends very normal.

*Share something silly you never thought you'd do (but obviously did or wanted to do!):*

*Kid:*_____

_____

_____

*Parents (from those teen years, please!):*_____

_____

_____

_____

What about the risky side of the teen brain—and that doesn't just mean when you are comfortable wearing a hot dog suit in public. Remember the 👵"Grandma Rule?" Don't post or text anything you wouldn't be able to show Grandma? This is one place this rule really comes in—yes, to show your faith, as stated before. So why mention it again? Because you are changing and going to change, and then probably change again. The developing brain in your teenage years doesn't quite have the full restraint (self-control) it will when you are an adult. You may need to **constantly** keep the "Grandma Rule" in mind. Why do you practice a layup? So when you have a breakaway during a game, you can perform and make the play. Why mention the "Grandma Rule"? So when you are experiencing emotional ups and downs and a lack of caution, you are prepared for the "tomorrow."

It's the same thought—be prepared. When you are frustrated at something or someone, you (and probably most adults) can think of several things you might want to say to the world or that person—this is a "stop-and-think" moment, like a manual override. For instance, a friend of mine, new to her profession, had an older coworker ream her out (no gentle questioning). She responded with, "Thanks for the input," and let the tears come later. I wondered if I would've defended myself or what I would've done in her situation. I've appreciated learning her response. I've used it in different situations since. You can't prepare for everything, but you can pick up key tips and advice along the way to help be prepared. And . . . remember one more thing: When you make choices (on your phone and otherwise) that [4ᵀᴴ] honor your father and mother (and Grandma), God promises to help your life go well, to bless you in ways beyond what you can imagine.

*So if you are frustrated with your friend's post online, maybe everyone is together without you, you could look at Grandma's picture and then respond:*

*Kid:*_____

_____

_____

*Parents (how you might respond or what you think your child could say):*_____

_____

_____

_____

*Parents and Kids*
*Let's gather a list of things that could use a "stop and think" before doing (I'll get you started with a few):*

Using your phone during school hours, "following" any celebrity (or possibly certain friends), texting while driving, playing games (especially with rating for violence, sexuality, etc.), online gaming with friends who use questionable language during play, "on demand" movies/TV programming, or really any of these that threaten to consume your time and attention . . .

_____

_____

_____

_____

_____

_____

_____

_____

Look back over the list and circle the one you (parent or kid) think is the most harmful (or harmful for you). Explain why you think that:

Kid's response: _____

_____

_____

_____

Parents' response: _____

_____

_____

_____

You cannot take your words back—EVER. You cannot take back a mean-spirited picture you posted—EVER. Apologies do happen, and posts can be removed. But as stated previously, the message or picture cannot be unseen. The power of self-restraint, of using a "stop and think," is invaluable.

You cannot change your stage of life, but you can go about it forewarned and armed with knowledge. Enjoy the stage of life you are in—the "today." King David declared in Psalm 139:14,

"I praise you because I am fearfully and wonderfully made." And so you are. Be silly and happy. Be real. Be authentic. AND, take responsibility for who you are. An 80-year-old with poor eyesight who causes a car accident can't push off the responsibility simply because she wanted to drive and can't help that she's losing her sight. Similarly, a teen can't push off responsibility for poorly thought-out actions because his or her brain is documented to be less cautious at that age. Paul gives us a good insight into this idea that we are accountable: "'I have the right to do anything,' you say—but not everything is beneficial. 'I have the right to do anything'—but not everything is constructive. No one should seek their own good, but the good of others" (1 Corinthians 10:23,24). It's kinda like when Mom left you at preschool and said, "Make good choices." We do what we do because we are children of God—loved and wanting to show our thanks, whatever our place or stage in this life (today affects tomorrow).

Sometimes the "stop and think" isn't just about what we actively *do* on phones, but it's also about what we *take in* with phones (stayed tuned for the next chapter).

*Knowing that the teenage years may make you less cautious, what are you looking forward to being more outgoing about and what things might you want to be cautious about (even though your brain might not!)?*

*Kid's thoughts:*_____

_____

_____

_____

*Parents' advice:*_____

_____

_____

_____

Think back to this previously mentioned fact: In a study about teens and cell phones, the kids surveyed said that parents have the *biggest* influence on what they will decide is appropriate or inappropriate behavior online (Lenhart et al.).

*With the help of your parents (reread above, if necessary), look back to what you listed above in the "stop and thinks" as harmful (especially to you), and start a plan for how you will manage your online decisions in the teenage stage:*

*Kid's response:* _____

_____

_____

*Parents' response:* _____

_____

_____

As for all those hairdos and styles that you were remembering and cringing over—don't worry. Solomon told us, "What has been will be again, what has been done will be done again; there is nothing new under the sun" (Ecclesiastes 1:9). God knows the cycles of life we face (and will face). The cycles may look different throughout the different centuries and decades. Study history and God's Word—you'll see evidence of the same joy, same jealousy, same love, same envy, and same lack of inhibition cycling through all time. It may take 30 years, but even styles recycle if you wait long enough—*closet space may be a problem though, if you are waiting for the styles to come back* ☺. Take comfort that there is something that is not ever going to be outdated—a loving God who is there to walk and guide you at every step, as he has been throughout all of history.

> Jesus Christ is the same
> yesterday and today and forever.
> (Hebrews 13:8)

# Real Life

### or
### What do empathy, silence, and conversation have in common?

*Kids and Parents:*

If you answered the title question with, "They all have an *e*," you would be correct. Even more, though, they are all connected as areas where people struggle socially. Need more help connecting the words? Silence and conversation are nearly opposites, yet *both* may send you fearfully running like you've seen a zombie apoca-  lypse coming (i.e. you want to avoid them, *and fyi, zombies aren't real either—feel free to take a moment if you need it*). And empathy, well, it isn't *necessarily* that people avoid it; it's just becoming a rarer trait.

*Empathy—how do you define it? (Hint, see the next paragraph.) If you can think of a real-life example of empathy, please share!*

*Kid's definition:*_____

_____

_____

_____

_____

*Parents' definition:*_____

_____

_____

_____

_____

Many would define empathy as being able to feel or understand what another person is feeling—to be able to "put yourself in someone else's shoes." Learning empathy often begins when children are young. You saw tears or a trembling lip, and you knew someone was hurting. You ask, "What's wrong," or, "Are you okay?" We learn to read faces and body movements—cues that show how another person is feeling.

**Story Time:** I remember my oldest daughter, not even two years old, comforting her grandma. We were at the funeral of grandma's father (my daughter's great-grandfather). My daughter went over to her crying grandma, hugged her, and said, "It's okay, Grandpa-in-the-box is in heaven, Grandma." At not even two, she could see the signs of hurt, so she hugged and comforted her grandma (and gave us some comic relief—"Grandpa-in-the-box"!).

People have different abilities in reading emotions. Generally, the more time you spend with certain people, the better you can read those people. I remember the first time a certain student came to me and tried to explain why he thought another student was upset with him. He described the other student as "looking at him with frowny eyebrows." I had never thought about how eyebrows may look when someone is angry or frustrated—or even happy for that matter. For me, the "language" of emotions wasn't difficult to understand. This certain student, however, needed to work with his therapist to understand what different facial expressions meant to understand and be empathetic about how others might be feeling.

*Can you remember a time when you were little when you comforted another person OR needed to be shown how someone else felt?*

*Kid's response:* _____
_____
_____
_____
_____
_____
_____

*Parents' response:* _____

_____

_____

_____

_____

_____

So what's empathy got to do with devices, anyway? People who regularly multitask (flip from thing to thing) on devices *may* be losing the ability to read emotions. In order to understand people and their emotions, people have to *spend time with people*. The more time we spend on devices, the less time we actually spend with people, and that effects how well we understand people (Cohen). A University of California, Los Angeles study isolated a group of sixth-graders for five days. The students were not able to access *any* electronic devices during the study. Afterwards, the scientists reported that the students were considerably better at reading other people's emotions than their peers were (Wolpert). It may seem strange to spend time and money just to study if people are lacking in empathy. Realize this: Something as seemingly unimportant as spending our free time on devices can affect our ability to communicate well with other people. Once again, the devices are neither good nor bad—really neutral—but how and how often we *use* these devices are what's important.

*How have you seen cell phones hurt empathy? Recall if you've seen people SO into their phone that they don't notice people. What did the cell phone user <u>do</u> or <u>not do</u> with the people he was ignoring around him—like not holding the door for a mom and child, etc.?*

*Kid's observation:* _____

_____

_____

_____

_____

_____

Parents' observation:_____

_____

_____

_____

_____

_____

*Can you think of other things that are "neutral," neither good nor bad, by themselves but can hurt us or others when used in excess?*

Kid's observation:_____

_____

_____

_____

Parents' observation:_____

_____

_____

_____

_____

So here's the big irony—we're spending time looking in on people digitally, but it is hurting our face-to-face abilities with people. And the ability to read emotions is not the only part of communicating that's being hurt. Again, we might be stunned that *"social"* media could be hurting our social skills. Sherri Turkle, a media researcher for over 30 years, again and again points to the *need* to multitask as one aspect that is hurting our social skills. Stop and think about the things you like to do on your cell phone: you might be checking social media, but then a text comes in, and you respond. Soon after, you see an article on your feed and you look it up, which then causes you to watch a linked video. You may switch over and check notifications for a moment, send a message, and then go back to your favorite browser to look up some random information. All these activities may just seem like random chilling, but eventually they can become huge time wasters and distractions from life. They may *also* unintentionally retrain your brain to always be picking up and dropping random information. Suddenly the brain is like a scavenger searching out whatever will hold its attention. Again, none of this may seem really bad; it certainly isn't an evil plan to cause the destruction of society. Part of the problem is that we are s-l-o-w-l-y retrained to think that life (and conversation) is led by dipping in and out as we *feel* like giving attention (Turkle). Certainly, life doesn't have to be endlessly boring—that we can *never* pay attention to what interests us—BUT there are going to be many parts of life that are not going to be super interesting. You may not be interested in the parts of speech or why we signed a treaty over a hundred years ago. But if we only make ourselves pay attention to things we like, then we are going to struggle again and again in necessary (possibly BORING) parts of life.

*\*\*\*Spoiler alert:* A lot of chores in adult life are not fun or exciting! Not only do some parts of life seem—well, let's be honest—boring, but the level of excitement of many of the games and online media is *so* high that *normal conversation or school instruction* seem boring in comparison (Prooday). This doesn't mean conversation or instruction IS really boring. We need to be careful not to have all our free time activities be at such extremely high levels that normal life feels boring! Video games and media multitasking feed the instant gratification monster of "**all**-I-want-**when**-I-want-it-**all**-the-time." Real life is not like having chocolate sundaes all the time (and that's what being on a cell phone 24/7 is like!).

*Do you think your brain is being retrained? Are you "jumping" all over online (and then in other parts of life?) Explain:*

Kid's response: _____

_____

_____

_____

Parents' response: _____

_____

_____

_____

Occupational therapists, those same people who help others read emotions, also urge us that we **need** to work the brain muscles that do *boring, repetitive things*. We need to learn to do things that are not fun, and not just flip to a different activity, web page, or social media platform every time it doesn't hold our attention anymore. Victoria Prooday, an occupational therapist, says, "To be able to delay gratification means to be able to function under stress. Our children are gradually becoming less equipped to deal with even minor stressors, which eventually become huge obstacles to their success in life." We have to learn to delay gratification because, well, it's reality that you can't just have *whatever* you want *whenever* you want it, and often we enjoy more the things we have to wait for. If you have to save up for something for a long time, you usually treasure (and anticipate) it more!

*Share times when you've had to wait for something (and how you felt, either waiting or when you got it):*

*Kid's response:* _____

_____

_____

_____

_____

*Parents' response:* _____

_____

_____

_____

_____

You may wonder, why even concern ourselves with all of this? We'll just limit the time we all spend on our devices. That may sound like a good plan, but it is not going to solve the problem. More and more, just to keep up with everyday life, we **need** to use the technological advances happening constantly. Students access grades, read books, and do classwork online. People track exercise and communicate online. We can't just *ignore* the age in which we live. However, multitasking—the feeding of instant gratification—and the possible lack of empathy that comes from it show us that we need to be more *aware* as we use cell phones and other devices.

These issues also lead to other social issues. Part of being empathetic is realizing that each person in the world is unique, has feelings, and is loved by God. Kids, your parents are **real** people who want to interact with you (and deserve your respect!). Parents, your children are trying to balance living in this techie age. The sea of seeming zombies at the mall **is** *really* made up of people *(we've already cleared up that zombies aren't real)*. Having phones everywhere, along with being busy and loving our instant gratification, has moved society to a point where people *are around people, but not **connected** to them.* Now, you don't suddenly need to set the phone down and start staring contests with everyone around you in an effort to look friendlier and more empathetic (that might freak them out). We do, however, need to realize and show that the *devices are not as important as the people holding the devices.* Think about this stat: "39% of millennials say they interact more with their smartphone than they do with their significant others, parents, friends, children or co-workers" (Hill). Yes, the phone may seem like more "fun" at times, but devices are **not** replacements for people.

*How can you appear (and actually be) more interested in people than in your phone? (Obviously you can put the phone away—any other thoughts? Smile at people, not run into them at the mall?)*

*Kid's response:* _____

_____

_____

*Parents' response:* _____

_____

_____

We've talked about regret—if we don't spend the time God's given us with the people we love, later in life we may feel loss. We've mentioned how hard it can be to put the phone down because the multitasking keeps us charmed and possibly *happier* than people can. Turkle noticed this in her years of studying media. She wrote, "I saw that computers offer the illusion of companionship. . . . Because, face-to-face, people ask for things computers never do" (Turkle). The reality is that talking with people *can* be boring at times. People cannot always give the excitement: they do not always change, like devices can change, when what they are doing is *not* really stimulating. People expect you to meet *their* needs. When you spend time with a person, a person needs you to respond, give eye contact and other signals that you are listening (ah, be empathetic?). Why even bother—why do we take the time to care about people? "We love because he first loved us" (1 John 4:19). We *bother* because Jesus loved us enough to die for us. We bother because God's love lives in us and motivates us to care about these people he loves. (And when we need the reminder—because as humans, we forget—we can read that Bible passage from a few sentences ago and remember *what* and *who* love is.)

*Think of someone you struggle to give attention to (or who maybe annoys you). How can you intentionally show care toward that person the next time you are talking?*

Kid's response: _____

_____

_____

_____

_____

Parents' response: _____

_____

_____

_____

_____

If you are one-on-one, you **can't** sit and rewrite an answer or take 20 pictures until you have the "right one." And that's another skill that soon becomes lacking, the ability to answer and communicate right now. Why? There is a loss of control; you aren't sitting in a "safe" environment, figuring out what to say or post. Emailing and texting appear "safer" to many because they eliminate the need to answer right away and pay attention to someone else. In fact, one article dares to ask, *"Teen Texting Soars; Will Social Skills Suffer?"* In the article, one teacher noted that students aren't afraid to be bold and confident in emails but often appear "shy and awkward" in person (Ludden). Teens even admitted they choose texting in order to avoid "confrontation or uncomfortable situations" (Ludden). Like anything else in life, **just because something is hard doesn't mean we don't do it! We need to work those skills even more.** Those communicating skills don't just magically appear at a person's first job interview, first date, or first public speech. The elementary student who doesn't practice his flash cards isn't somehow able to perform long division without errors, and neither should **we** expect to be able to communicate well in conversation if we never work at it!

*Think of times you had to talk to someone (even though you secretly wanted to crawl under the table), and share!*

Kid's response: _____

_____

_____

Parents' response: _____

_____

_____

Texting seems easier because you also can't see the effect it has on the other person. You have *time* to respond or *reword* your responses. Part of using that empathy skill is actually seeing the effect that words of love, comfort, or even confrontation have. It takes courage to face problems in person, but that is a healthy step of being human. Texting (and messaging and emailing) certainly has a place and can be a wonderful time-saver and long-distance tool. However, it is important to think through what kinds of conversations are better to have in person.

*What kinds of conversations are better in person?*
*(For instance, "Can I borrow . . ." vs. "I'm sorry I broke your tablet . . .")*

Kid's response: _____

_____

_____

_____

_____

Parents' response: _____

_____

_____

_____

_____

Sometimes it's not even that people don't want to talk to others. You might love being around people. The problem might be what's in your hand. The famous saying of Rene Descartes, "I think, therefore I am," might be better translated for today as, "I have a device, therefore I check it." We've already stated that many people like having a phone because they feel safer in case something bad should *"tragically befall"* them—am I exaggerating too much?! Phones surely are wonderful for times of flat tires, cancelled plans, and, oh yeah, *real* emergencies. But the reality is that just having a phone handy may actually drive us to check the phone, and then, "I just lost touch with the world around me for the last 15 minutes."

The *presence* of the phone can actually affect how we converse with others. In fact, in studies of people's conversation, people generally keep the conservation lighter just because there is a cell phone present (Turkle). The thought that a phone might interrupt a conversation keeps people from reaching a deeper level of conversation—<u>even</u> *when the phone is powered off!* On the flip side, studies show having the phone **gone** during conversation boosted empathy levels (Misra et al.). Think about this: (1) we connect better without the possibility of a distraction (and we do know how interesting devices can be!); and (2) maybe it's already hard enough to put yourself "out there," and now you have to compete with a cell phone?! What girl wants to pour her heart out, only to be second to the updated NFL score of *his* favorite team?

*Have you ever felt ignored because someone gave more attention to a device than you? Share:*

*Kid's response:* _____
_____
_____
_____
_____
_____

*Parents' response:* _____
_____
_____
_____
_____
_____

**Story Time:** During a presentation I attended, I observed the people around me. Ironically, many were not actually "attending" *(attending here meaning we give our attention to something)*. I noticed around me that some people were taking notes and answering or asking questions, but many were checking social media, emails, etc. I couldn't help but wonder about that. I can't say I never check my phone—I would periodically check and make sure no one had sent a "911" text or called me. (I have actually had instances of needing to give information back and forth for medical emergencies and such.) In contrast to needing to give medical info to my family, many were obviously—right in front of the presenter—surfing the web, multitasking, and "liking." I actually felt bad for the presenter. Who wants to compete with *that*—a phone of infinite possibilities?!

At break time most took out devices and checked in. Again, something struck me as I looked around the room. Some did this privately, in a way that excused that person from the others around him or her, by looking down, or removing him- or herself from the group, even in some small way. Some people picked up their phones, held them in front of themselves, and continued to scroll through whatever was on their screens. It didn't bother me that they were on their devices (as I said, I've checked my phone before too!). As I looked around the room, though, I really wondered if any of them was aware that they could be *unintentionally sending this message:* "I am with you, but right now what I want to look at is more important than talking to the people around me." Make a connection with someone you haven't seen for a while? Nope. Get to know someone new at your table—a real, live human being? Nope. Discuss what you may have learned or what others thought of the presentation? Nope. Look at something on your phone that you'll probably forget about entirely in 45 minutes? Yes.

*Putting your cell phone in front of you like a shield will probably keep you from having to or getting to talk with those around you, but what will you miss? You can quickly catch up on updated statuses on the ride home, but <u>what are you missing by not connecting with the people around you</u>?*

*Kid's response:* _____

_____

_____

*Parents' response:* _____

_____

_____

*Are we more "person"able without our phones (we appear to be more real—authentic—people when we put the phone down)? Why/how?*

*Kid's response:* _____

_____

_____

*Parents' response:* _____

_____

_____

*Why might it be easier to communicate without having to compete against the phone for the "I'm-more-interesting-than-what-you-can-look-at-on-the-phone" award? (In other words, why might it be easier to talk without a phone nearby?)*

*Kid's response:* _____

_____

_____

_____

*Parents' response:* _____

_____

_____

_____

If you're used to being on a phone and multitasking like a running engine, it might make you frightened of silence. What??? Have you ever noticed what happens at stoplights, in the checkout lines, and any places people may be without (and sometimes with) friends? *People are checking devices.* You can justify yourself by thinking you are just getting up-to-date on emails or messages (or social media), but the reality is that people are often really afraid of (or not used to) doing nothing. Checking your phone *could* just be a really good use of time, but it's fairly safe to say that **no one** needs *every* free minute to "catch up." In fact, researchers in a study of confinement (that means no phone, no other people, . . . nothing) observed that people would rather do something **harmful** to themselves *than do **nothing***—the people in the study chose to give themselves electric shocks rather than do nothing! (Wilson et al.). Seem pretty extreme?

*Reflect: What would you possibly be doing during "down time"—when you are stuck in line, waiting at a stoplight (and if you couldn't use your phone, like in the study above)?*

Kid's response: _____

_____

_____

_____

Parents' response: _____

_____

_____

_____

Not only are other people (family/friends) possibly put off to the side by constantly being "on" technology, so also can our spiritual relationship go to the side. If you choose to spend most of your time, energy, and interest on a device, it could potentially become your new "god." Anything we adore more than God—our sports, our relaxation, even our family—have the potential to become an idol (something that takes the place of God as first in our lives). Psalm 5:3 says, "In the morning, LORD, you hear my voice; in the morning I lay my requests before you and wait expectantly." But it isn't just mornings when priorities matter. We want to *use* this wonderful technology but not *bow* at its altar. A phone is a gift from God. It can be used to show God to the world, but a phone will never save us from anything other than boredom (and *that* still needs to be done by the operator of the device—the phone is still just a thing!).

*How could the world be different if we spent even half the time we spend on our devices in prayer for other people?*

Kid's response: _____

_____

_____

Parents' response: _____

_____

_____

We often turn to the phone not just for boredom or entertainment but to distract ourselves from stress and disappointments. What else could we do? Suggestions: Find a few Bible verses here to memorize or type into a "notes" app (or have a Bible app and have those verses highlighted!). Find a real person, especially a mom or dad type! Easily an awesome choice—pray to God, who is definitely available always!

*Which are some of the ways or Bible verses from this book (or that you know) that you could use to help you handle life?*

Kid's response: _____

_____

_____

Parents' response: _____

_____

_____

We can see all the pieces in this puzzle of interacting with each other like a jigsaw puzzle. Each piece has a place in our lives, as puzzle pieces always do. Piece 1: We have a responsibility to see the people around us—they're not just decorations in the backdrop of life. Piece 2: We have technology to use responsibly (what we look at, how long we look). Piece 3: We need to take time to understand who we are—parents or children, servants of our Savior. Finally, the table the puzzle sits on: Adults/parents have a responsibility to practice what they preach (not "do as I say, not as I do") with technology. So let's look at the current habits out there (maybe even our own habits).

*Do I take out a device while other people are talking if I am not interested in the conversation? (For instance, Mom is talking to others in a public place—is it okay for anyone else to take out his or her phone and ignore what's going on?)*

Kid's response: _____

_____

_____

Parents' response: _____

_____

_____

As a team, decide if this is okay in your family, or when it is okay and when it is not.

Kid's response: _____

_____

_____

Parents' response: _____

_____

_____

What about those "we're-not-really-doing-anything" times, like waiting on the soccer practice sidelines, etc.?

Kid's response: _____

_____

_____

Parents' response: _____

_____

_____

Are there times even during the "okay" times that you should look up and <u>try</u> to make conversation because there are people around (remember being empathetic?)? (Like, "Can I ignore the people at <u>every</u> game I have to sit through for my little sister, or should I try to be personable for part of the time?")

Kid's response: _____

_____

_____

Parents' response: _____

_____

_____

We've probably all been somewhere while someone was loudly talking on a phone even though there were people all around. Or we've seen a couple or a parent and child out together, but they were <u>definitely</u> not taking time to talk to each other (and are possibly all on devices). Does this make you think of other times <u>when</u> and <u>where</u> it is a better choice to put the device away?

Kid's response: _____

_____

_____

Parents' response: _____

_____

_____

As you grow up, you need to be able to perform jobs or tasks to succeed and earn an income. You will need the ability to focus—again, this could be a possible problem if multitasking from thing to thing becomes a habit! In higher levels of education, it varies whether you can use a phone or device during instruction periods. Many students use computers for taking notes, but that could bring the desire to multitask, which distracts from your learning. Down the road, assuming you work at being a conversationalist (hint, hint—*talk to people*), you may interview for and land a job. That job might be mowing lawns, it might be babysitting, or you may dream of becoming a doctor, teacher, or nurse.

Whether you are babysitting, working at a store, or are a doctor, does it matter if you are texting or internet surfing on the job?

Kid's response: _____

_____

_____

Parents' response: _____

_____

_____

*When do you think it matters and why?*

Kid's response: _____

_____

_____

Parents' response: _____

_____

_____

*And does it matter if <u>someone else is doing the surfing and texting on the job</u> vs. <u>you</u> doing the surfing and texting on the job?*

Kid's response: _____

_____

Parents' response: _____

_____

Whenever we choose to look at a phone or other media devices, we are choosing not to give our full attention to the task in front of us. As a parent, you may not want someone you are paying to watch your children to be texting. A babysitter may feel that it doesn't matter as long as the children are safe and reasonably happy. You may feel that different jobs require different levels of attention—or maybe that what you are paid plays into whether it's okay (less pay, less attention?). There certainly *are* differences in the attention to detail of certain jobs, but the bottom line is that a *job is something you are paid to do.* Therefore, you need to make good choices as to whether you should be on your phone or not (or ask if you aren't sure it's acceptable). As a teacher, I inform parents that I will *periodically* check messages—this helps keep the connection open that Chloe's lunch is late but Grandma will drop it off, or Aunt Allison is picking up Chase. This does NOT give me license to be checking social media or playing online games during the school day (or even looking constantly at my phone!). There are no one-size-fits-all rules for all jobs, but again, if you are really unsure, asking is better than assuming and looking bad with your employer! Also, we as phone users need to note that any of us may appear two-faced if we think it is fine for *us* to use the phone—because we have good reasons, etc.—but other people should not be using their phones on the job. A job means we are paid for our time and work (and not to check our social media platforms).

Food for thought: In 2010, a shocking report shared that over half of the 439 perfusionists *(people who help keep heart patients alive)* surveyed had admitted to using a cell phone in some manner (texting, checking social media, etc.) during a cardiopulmonary bypass (heart surgery!) (Smith).

> *You may not think of checking the latest message as "hurtful" to whatever other job you are performing. Is it okay to be looking at a phone while being paid to keep someone alive?! Thoughts:*
>
> *Kid's response: _____*
>
> *_____*
>
> *Parents' response: _____*
>
> *_____*

Assignment: Parents and kids, spend some time together and talk without the phone nearby. You can talk about anything—sports, friends, your life's dream. *The point is to talk without a phone nearby.* See if you can still read each other's faces and emotions, and then practice empathy as you listen. *Actually* listen—because you care. Kids, listen because you want to honor your parents (and that will bless you!). Use those skills—they can help you today and in the future! Pssst . . . it's okay if some of the time you sit together is silent—that's a sign you are comfortable together!

Let the peace of Christ
rule in your hearts,
since as members of one body
you were called to peace. . . .
And whatever you do, whether in word or deed,
do it all in the name of the Lord Jesus,
giving thanks to God the Father through him.
(Colossians 3:15,17)

# What's the Harm, Anyway?

## Part I—
## Internal Harms—Health, Education, Contentment, Focus, Anxiety

*Kids and Parents:*

A doctor visit—most likely you have an annual checkup planned every year. You work around the insurance guidelines, and it usually ends up being around your birthday every year. The doctor asks how you are. He (or she) asks what sports you are doing, how your eating habits are, and if you have firearms in the house. He asks you what your favorite color is—*no, wait, that's your kindergarten teacher* 😊. In recent years, doctors have added another section of questions to the list: they ask about your media habits. Specifically, the American Academy of Pediatrics (AAP) encourages all doctors to ask two questions: "How much recreational screen time does your child or teenager consume daily? Is there a television set or internet-connected device in the child's bedroom?" Why do doctors care about media use? Although we don't fully know the possible future problems of overusing media, we do have some clues that show we should be cautious. It's kind of like eating candy. Candy is out there and readily available. In theory, you could eat candy for every meal. We probably don't have data for anyone who's done that, but we can guess how much it would hurt your body over time if you only ate candy. You would likely start to look and feel unhealthy, which would start affecting the other parts of your life (becoming cranky, irritable, unable to pay attention well, soaring from sugar-high to sugar-low, and so on . . . ).

So what could be the harm of too much media time? Whether it's fears about the developing brain, or fears that media use can cause delayed development, obesity, aggression, attention deficit, addictions, or even harm from radiation, doctors are paying attention (National Institute for Mental Health; Rowan). Do you ever listen to commercials for prescription drugs, and by the time the announcer is done listing all the possible side effects, you wonder if people would be safer just **not** taking them? (Or at least you pray that you don't ever have to choose between taking on the side effects or just suffering the illness!) What if every phone commercial ended with an announcer quickly reading, "Not every cell phone user may experience these symptoms, but some cell phone/multimedia users have been reported to experience possibly harmful side effects to the developing brain. Although unknown, it may also lead to obesity, aggression, mental illness, internet or other addictions, and uncertain harm from potential radiation. Never use your cell phone without first contacting your doctor for a plan of use"? Would we **then** look at cell phones and media use differently???

*Which of those possible media side effects is the most alarming to you? Why?*

*Kid's response:* _____

_____

_____

_____

*Parents' response:* _____

_____

_____

_____

Parents: So how do you take the doctor's advice for cell phones? Remember moderation—like eating candy, you don't need to ban it, but just use it in moderation. But what *is* moderation for cell phone use? The AAP encourages kids ages 2-18 to limit total entertainment time to 🕑 two hours a day. Note that amount is termed "entertainment time." That time would NOT include writing and researching papers for school, etc. The AAP also encourages parents to see what their child is viewing on devices and watch movies and videos with them. Awkward? Maybe. Uncomfortable? It probably is some of the time. Be honest—those are never great excuses to avoid talking about real life. Those possibly uncomfortable viewing moments are often the timeliest opportunities to point out what is NOT a good example in movies and videos. You probably can't sit and watch every little thing together, but be honest about which shows are good choices and why. Don't know? Use sites like commonsensemedia.org and others to find input on the content and viewer level. Parents, look back and remember other uncomfortable times: the vaccine shots or the endless crying in the car seat—when all you wanted to do was comfort or take the place of your child. Is this really any different? Was it harder to endure the crying for hours than it is to sit together and watch programming and trending videos?

*What were some of those hard moments when your child was younger?*

*Parents' response:* _____

_____

_____

_____

*Where do you see opportunities to keep sharing and teaching (even through the hard and awkward times)?*

*Parents' response:* _____

_____

_____

Kids: What if your cell phone habits and use became toxic in a different way? What if they became harmful to your education? We could add to the doctor's list, "And heavy use may cause a sudden drop in grades" (but more importantly, your education!). The Kaiser Family Foundation conducted a study of the media habits of 8- to 18-year-olds. Their goal was not only to see what kids are doing with the media but also how it is shaping and affecting them. One interesting point they noted, although it is not a clear-cut, cause-effect issue, is that "youth who spend more time with media report lower grades and lower levels of personal contentment" (Rideout et al.). Think back to how much time you "guesstimated" you spend on media and how much you think you actually do use. This study grouped the youth into groups of heavy, moderate, and light media users. "Heavy users are those who consume more than 16 hours of media content in a typical day (21% of all 8- to 18-year-olds); moderate users are those who consume from 3–16 hours of content (63%); light users are those who consume less than three hours of media in a typical day (17%). Nearly half (47%) of all heavy media users say they usually get fair or poor grades (mostly C's or lower), compared to 23% of light media users" (Rideout et al.). There are always going to be exceptions to the rule in any situation, but the facts seemed to fairly **shout** that while some media time may be okay, high amounts affect your grades.

Do grades even matter? Remember that even your abilities are gifts from God! When you try to the best of your ability, you can be saying thank you to God and faithfully "managing" your gifts from him! You are also making good use of the *time* that God has given you and of the nice *teachers* God has put in your life. *(You've probably liked one or two, or all of them?)* So, yes, grades do matter! (And it especially matters that the grades reflect *your* ability, not anyone else's!) Also, you honor your parents by working as hard as you have the ability to—which will help you reach your potential in life and help you find joy when you're all grown-up yourself. (Mind if I quote that Bible promise again? "'Honor your father and mother'—which is the first commandment with a promise—'so that it may go well with you and that you may enjoy long life on the earth'" (Ephesians 6:2,3). Enjoying long life because you tried hard in school the way your parents wanted you to? Honoring your parents and being blessed? Almost as good as chocolate.)

*Kids: Write down blessings that come to you and others by working hard in school (in a way that really thanks God and parents).*

_____

_____

_____

*Think about it: Has your phone/media time ever caused your grades to be less than they could be or hurt your ability to play sports or pay attention? If so, how? (Or how have you seen it affect others?)*

*Kid's response:* _____

_____

_____

_____

Go back to that stat a couple of paragraphs ago about how 21% of young people spend more than 16 hours a day in front of a screen. What things would a person need to give up in order to do *anything* for more than 16 hours a day? Would you give up sleep? time with people? normal meals? education? You can't stretch time—it exists in the same amount no matter how you use it. If you give up 16 hours a day to be on media, by the set rules of time, you *have* to give up something else.

*What are the normal things people do every day?*

*Kid's response:* _____

_____

_____

*Parents' response:* _____

_____

_____

*Any thoughts about people giving up 16 hours of normal life to be on a device? Is it crazy? harmful? reckless? fun? Explain:*

*Kid's reaction:* _____

_____

_____

_____

_____

_____

_____

*Parents' reaction:*_____

_____

_____

_____

_____

_____

Sadly enough, as mentioned earlier with FOMO, being on media excessively can have the unwanted side effect of actually making people *unhappy*. People seek media to fill that empty feeling, hoping the activities create feelings of happiness. Unfortunately, it often has the *opposite effect:* people compare their lives to a screen version of others and become discontent. "Heavy media users are also more likely to say they get into trouble a lot, are often sad or unhappy, and are often bored" (Rideout et al.).

*Any thoughts on why someone doing what he or she "wants"*
*(being on a device) all day long might actually make him or*
*her <u>more unhappy, sad, or bored</u>?*

*Kid's thoughts:*_____

_____

_____

*Parents' thoughts:*_____

_____

_____

Interestingly, those surveyed who felt the highest levels of content-ment ***also*** spent ***less*** time on media *(compared to people spending more time on media and still not being content).*

*How can people maintain a "good amount" of screen time*
*without going over the line?*

*Kid's thoughts:*_____

_____

_____

_____

*Parents' thoughts:*_____

_____

_____

Here's something we talked about a little before: Media use may not only be hurting grades and contentment levels, but it may also be harming children's ability to pay attention. A child who can't pay attention will struggle more in school. Victoria Prooday explains, "Compared to virtual reality, everyday life is boring." Children who constantly view fast-paced video games and other media are actually *reshaping* their forming brains to process information in different ways, and it's not necessarily for the better. "Processing information in a classroom becomes increasingly challenging for our kids because their brains are getting used to the high levels of stimulation that video games provide. The inability to process lower levels of stimulation leaves kids vulnerable to academic challenges" (Prooday).

*Kid's thoughts:*_____

_____

_____

*\*Do you see kids (or even yourself) so used to a faster pace ("video game speed") that it's hard to pay attention?*

_____

_____

*\*What do they (or you) have to do to pay attention? (fidget devices, drawing?)*_____

_____

_____

_____

*Parents' thoughts:*_____

_____

_____

Studies show that phones might be making us more anxious too. A California State University, Dominquez Hills study suggests "our phones are keeping us in a continual state of anxiety in which the only antidote—is the phone" (Cooper). Part of the reason you may see kids and adults checking their phones so often may be related to feelings of anxiety. Most people probably wouldn't say they feel anxious, but the studies show that levels of cortisol (the chemical we release when we are stressed) often rise when a person hasn't checked his or her phone. That need to check the phone is anxiety, and the stress is released by checking the phone. Here's how it can start: You get a phone, you check your phone, you start checking your phone A LOT, you feel that you need to keep checking your phone (a habit is created)—so you do, and then you have a NEED to check the phone (anxiety). One action led to another and suddenly a habit of checking the phone or feeling stressed is created. Every time you release the stress by checking the phone you might get hooked to look at a notification or play something, and then you've been sucked in just to ease those anxious feelings. (That just sounds stressful!)

"67% of cell owners find themselves checking their phone for messages, alerts, or calls—even when they don't notice their phone ringing or vibrating" (Pew Research Center, "Mobile Fact Sheet"). In other words, there probably isn't anything new on their phones, but they feel the need to check them anyway.

*What could you do to keep yourself from getting sucked into the "anxiety/check phone" cycle? (Put the phone somewhere nearby but not "on" you? Put it in another room? Have times when you turn it off?)*

*Kid's ideas:*_____

_____

_____

*Parents' ideas:*_____

_____

_____

*Parents (especially):*
Are you seeing that too much of a good thing is no longer a good thing?! **That** may even beg the question, Would most of what we do with phones be deemed *good* things or activities? The Bible urges

us to spend our time thinking about things that are noble, right, lovely—even excellent or praiseworthy (Philippians 4:8). As we guide our children in "good uses" of these tools or gifts from God, we may struggle answering, "How much time will be right?" Start by just setting a boundary and then negotiate it as needed to make everyone comfortable (or as comfortable as is possible when negotiating limits!). You might feel more empowered knowing that a study further noted that "children who live in homes that limit media opportunities spend less time with media. For example, kids whose parents *don't* put a TV in their bedroom, *don't* leave the TV on during meals or in the background when no one is watching, or *do* impose some type of media-related rules spend substantially less time with media than do children with more media-lenient parents" (Foehr). That may seem like common sense to most people, but kids *really are* looking to parents to set the rules. If you don't put it in front of them, they aren't as likely to use it! Rules and boundaries make kids feel safe, even if their reaction seems to say opposite at times. Placing boundaries says "I love you enough" to toe the line, to show I care, to make you upset if necessary—but you'll thank me later. In fact, children might not outright say it, but they often appreciate having a boundary on when they can use their phones. It allows them to take a break from being available 24/7—that may sound odd, but a person who struggles to say no to peers (or self!) appreciates having Mom or Dad set the boundary (Gross).

*How can having a boundary of <u>when, how long, and how much I can use the phone</u> help both kids and parents? (And how might it work at your house?):*

*Kid's thoughts:*_____

_____

_____

*Parents' thoughts:*_____

_____

_____

Also, think into the future. Kids, you may have boundaries right now that your parents help you set, but even adults need God-pleasing boundaries. Being an adult doesn't mean I can ignore life to be on my phone/device whenever I want—I still have responsibilities. Having boundaries early in life trains you for when you are older and STILL need boundaries. Previously, the Bible passage mentioned spending our time on noble or praiseworthy things. Being a Christian adult means that even in my free time I won't just watch **any** on-demand movie or TV show or play online games which could have questionable content, have people playing using foul language, or be time-leeches. The boundaries aren't just for kids; the boundaries are to honor God.

*What are some online activities that may be popular but aren't the best choices for honoring God (and parents)?*

*Kid's thoughts:*_____

_____

_____

*Parents' thoughts:*_____

_____

_____

*Discuss your feelings about these popular online activities (whether you use it or just know others who do):*

*The "good/bad/or other" of them:*

*Kid's thoughts:*_____

_____

_____

_____

*Parents' thoughts:*_____

_____

_____

_____

Kids, remember that your parents are training you for God-pleasing future choices. This doesn't mean they are sheltering you, but rather they are training you to make good choices even when they aren't there to look over your shoulder! That's love!

# Part II:
# External Harms—
# Cyberbullying and Predators

*After noting all the potential problems cell phones/media access can cause, why did you decide to get a cell phone in the first place?*

*Kid's response:* _____

_____

_____

*Parents' response:* _____

_____

_____

*Parents mostly (Kids, read along):*

Reasons will vary from person to person and family to family for getting phones, but most people will point to having it for safety. The Pew Research Center documents that "for the most part, teens and adults share similar attitudes towards their cell phones. Both adults and teens nearly unanimously state (91% of adults and 93% of teens) that their cell phone makes them feel safer because they can always use it to get help" (Lenhart). Adults like the idea that they can contact their children at almost any time and in almost any place. Kids seem to like the safety aspect, but honestly, being able to connect with friends and the outside world is what makes the phone a powerful tool. And therein may lie one more potential harm. We convince ourselves that phones make us safer—but depending on what is done with the phone, your fingertips may be bringing you harm. This harm is often ***not even about you***. Phones are often harmful because of other people, sites, games, etc. How so? Having access to the internet, to games, to social media, and apps brings dangerous things to you—and you and your child may not be ready for that. In the article "Is Your Child Ready for a Cell Phone?" the author states, "Social interaction can be positive. It's one way kids can learn to relate to other kids. But there is also the potential for 'cyber bullying,' which is social harassment via text, instant messaging, or other social media. Many smartphones have a 'location sharing' feature, which could raise concerns about people stalking kids as they go from place to place" (Davis). And so on. Suddenly it may feel like giving a cell phone to your child is like opening Pandora's Box. If you remember the myth, Pandora's curiosity led her to open a box that let all kinds of terrible things out into the world. Sadly, the only thing that remained in the box was hope. You may feel torn between the fact that kids in the modern world are just "supposed to" have phones, but it is still your job to protect and guide your child to navigate and make good choices (in other words, not lose hope when you activate the phone!).

*Is a phone a bottomless pit of problems? What are some problems you've had or heard of from your friends (other parents)? (Friend requests from unknown players on games? Inappropriate language from players/users?)*

Kid's reaction/input:_____

_____

_____

_____

_____

_____

Parents' reaction/input:_____

_____

_____

_____

_____

_____

The reality is that parents need to be informed about what kids are doing, and kids and parents need to keep the lines of communication open—regardless of how awkward it may seem. Some parents install monitoring software on children's devices. Others recommend "following" your child if he or she is on social media. Your child may feel like this crosses the line on his or her privacy. On the other side, there are thousands of people (good, bad, or creepy) who could potentially contact your child through social media, and having you, his or her main advocate watching out is a step towards *safety,* not a privacy issue. And in the end, if loving your child enough to help keep him or her safe makes your child annoyed, that just might be another notch in your badge of tough love <3.

*What do you think about parents seeing what kids have done on their phones and being connected on social media?*

Kid's reaction:_____

_____

_____

_____

_____

_____

Parents' reaction:_____

_____

_____

_____

_____

_____

### Kids (and Parents):

Food for thought: Where's the line between secrecy and privacy? As in, if you don't feel like opening up about what you do with your phone, when does that stop being your privacy and become what looks like things you are doing in secret? So, yes, your privacy is always important, but—be aware that by *not wanting to share what you are doing* you may give the *appearance* that you are doing something you shouldn't be doing. (And honestly, as a child, you are, well . . . the child. You don't really have a right to keep your parents out.) One mom shared, "I'd say parents should definitely have access to who and when their kids are playing online."

*My Privacy vs. Secrecy—Where's the boundary, and how do we respect each other through it?*

*Kid's reaction:*_____

_____

_____

_____

_____

*Parents' reaction:*_____

_____

_____

_____

_____

Again, sometimes the harm in having a phone is really **not about you at all**. You may be sooooo careful with what you post and write, and people will **still** be mean for the sake of being mean. Sin is ugly in every form, and with every wave of new technology, sin will follow. People have been mean—taunting, bullying—since sin entered the world; we just now have a new medium for people to bully through. This medium never has to sleep and can reach a massive audience in milliseconds.

*"Bad news travels fast"—have you seen this with movie stars, politics, or in your own life?*

*Kid's response:* _____

_____

_____

_____

*Parents' response:* _____

_____

_____

_____

*Parents (and Kids):*

How do you protect your child from an enemy you may never see or be able to confront? Having information is a good starting point. The US government has launched sites to help you become proactive. They encourage parents to install monitoring devices (if you feel it's appropriate—explain it doesn't mean you need to look at everything they do), help check settings on apps for who can see posted information, explain what photos or videos shouldn't be uploaded ("Grandma Rule"), know what your child is doing online, and most importantly, make sure your child lets you know if he or she is being cyberbullied (USA.gov; stopbullying.gov). Some children will not report cyberbullying because they fear kickback from the bully, having devices taken away, or that he or she somehow caused this to happen in the first place. *Parents cannot protect and help if they do not know there is a problem.* Teach your child that your role as parent doesn't only exist on the good and ho-hum days, but also on the bad, dark, and downright awful days (*even* if he or she is knee-deep in helping to cause the problem).

*What measures have you taken together or will you now look at for becoming and staying safe?*

*Kid's response:* _____

_____

_____

_____

_____

_____

*Parents' response:* _____

_____

_____

_____

_____

_____

Pew Research reports:

"88% of social media-using teens have seen someone be mean or cruel on a social network site" (Lenhart et al.).

"One in five (21%) social media-using teens who have witnessed online cruelty say they have joined in" (Lenhart et al.).

*Have you witnessed or heard of people being mean or cruel on social media?*

*Kid's response:* _____
_____
_____
_____
_____
_____

*Parents' response:* _____
_____
_____
_____
_____

*Have you joined in, even a little, or witnessed online meanness or cruelty but didn't do anything?*

*Kid's response:* _____
_____
_____

*Parents' response:* _____
_____
_____

If, if, if cyberbullying happens? Don't respond or spread messages, keep all evidence (don't delete, and take a screenshot if necessary), and block the bully (stopbullying.gov). State laws may differ over what is considered a cyberbullying crime, but any time there are threats of violence, explicit photos/photos from places of privacy, or stalking/hate crimes, they should be reported to the proper authorities (stopbullying.gov). Ignoring an offender may seem like the safer or easier option, but many offenders will then just continue or even be driven to increase their pattern of crime. God has given us our government in order to help protect us so that we can live in peace.

### Kids (Parents)

Is bullying always clear-cut and always done by kids who are obviously heading down the road to juvie hall? No. "Mirror, mirror on the wall, who's the fairest one of all?" has quickly become, "Selfie, selfie, shown for all, climb the social ladder, tall." The power of becoming socially "on top" can be a powerful drug. Like any other sin, it is easy to convince yourself that you aren't doing anything wrong. The desire for "likes" can create a social ladder where one never has to actually look bad or face others. Insecurity of being at the bottom, or not making it to the top, may drive people to step over the line, be mean, or hurt people they normally wouldn't (and most definitely would not in person!). The point is not to label people as "bullies" suddenly but to be aware that "good" people and friends may cross the line—**you** may cross the line (or come close) in an attempt to be funny, make yourself look better, or because you didn't think through what you actually said.

The main point, though, is to remember that your true confidence will always come from a way-different change in the social ladder, a change that already happened. It comes from your Savior, who gave up perfection (not even a carefully cropped, seeming perfection, but actual perfection) to head to the absolute bottom of the ladder. You don't gain your confidence from being at the top or at the bottom of the social ladder—it comes from being loved by your Savior. Will it hurt if you are a target? Definitely. Your parents are there to help you through it. Your confidence doesn't need to be shaken; you have a Savior who suffered humiliation, torture, and hell—yet came out triumphantly. He will be there with you, should you go to the top, the bottom, or the in-between of the social ladder. He will stay at your side through it all and bring you closer to him, as all problems in this life can work to do. "We know that in all things God works for the good of those who love him," (Romans 8:28). No problem is too big for God, who has promised, 📖 "My grace is sufficient for you, for my power is made perfect in weakness" (2 Corinthians 12:9). Again, whether emotionally or socially you are low, high, or in-between, you have the confidence that God goes with you.

*Have you seen kids pushing the line to look better on the social ladder? What does it look like? How can your actions help make this worse? (How may you have done this yourself?)*

Kid's response: _____

_____

_____

_____

_____

Parents' response: _____

_____

_____

_____

_____

Unfortunately, living in a sinful world, a simple device like a phone can become one more way to hurt others or be hurt by others. As mentioned, most people (kids and adults) feel safer having a cell phone. How do the "good guys" and the "bad guys" weigh in on this?

## The "Bad Guys"

Scary but true, finding children and teens by using a phone is a predator's dream. The days are gone where just physically watching over a person can keep him or her safe. The World Wide Web connects through the walls that *used* to keep a child safe. Parents warn: Only connect with people you know! Many apps are designed to actually *help* you connect to strangers who are nearby. These are great features for people who want to stay up on what everyone else is doing (FOMO, anyone?). It's also a really easy way for predators to find, target, and "friend" young people. Predators often create fake profiles and then search for victims to prey upon. If it seems this is like something from those evening crime shows, it's not. In the end, the fortunate victims are those who report the activity to the police and parents before anything could happen (Ferman). The predators are **real,** and they have no qualms about following, stalking, or gathering material about kids to use later for blackmailing or other darker purposes. Be **aware** of who follows you, be careful what you post (not *just* because of the 👵 "Grandma Rule" but to show love and 📋 respect for God and parents), and don't be afraid to hurt someone's feelings by ignoring requests from people you don't know!

*Who do you consider safe to "follow" you or message with?*
*Kid's response:* _____

_____

_____

_____

_____

*Parents' response:* _____

_____

_____

_____

_____

## The "Good Guys"

*Parents (kids too):*
School policies about cell phone use vary from school to school. Some schools will allow students to have phones, but they must not be visible and must be turned off. Some schools require students to turn phones in during class. The general agreement is that phones distract from learning (at the very least) and are definitely a temptation to use when students need to focus. Many students have phones so they can contact parents after school or sports *(or the ever-important fast-food run?)*. The reality is that a school phone is always available for use, but most parents agree that the instant availability with a cell phone is a nicer option. There

*are* times, however, when the 📱 National School Safety and Security Services note that using cell phones is **not** a good idea, even though many would think otherwise. *In a crisis situation,* student use of cell phones could actually make the problems worse in two critical ways. If students choose to use their phones during a crisis, the cell phone system could become overloaded; and, more importantly, parents rushing to the school could actually *hinder the safety responders* from effectively carrying out their needed response or evacuation (or even cause parents to enter a dangerous area!) (National School Safety and Security Services). Even if your first reaction was, "Yes, but I need to know anytime my child is in harm's way!" Consider all sides. Parents trust teachers, administrators, and safety responders to take proper care of students every day (not to mention the almighty God, who is constantly watching over all of them!). These people are *trained* for emergencies, especially in that setting. Unless you are currently in one of the above listed roles during an emergency, you could be *preventing help*—all because of *your* NEED to be connected. Trust is often easy in theory but harder to put to the test!

*How might your thoughts about emergency cell phone use have changed?*

*Kid's reaction:*_____

_____

_____

_____

_____

_____

*Parents' reaction:*_____

_____

_____

_____

_____

_____

# One Last Potential Harm

*Parents: After reading all the possible harms, do you
see the harm in NOT communicating and establishing
boundaries (even if it makes your child frustrated today
vs. the harm of tomorrow if you <u>don't</u> use tough love)?
Tough love is helpful because . . .*

_____

_____

_____

_____

_____

📖 **"The one who loves their children is careful to discipline them"** (Proverbs 13:24).

📖 **"No discipline seems pleasant at the time, but painful. Later on, however, it produces a harvest of righteousness and peace for those who have been trained by it"** (Hebrews 12:11).

*Kids: Your last potential harm? Not seeing your parents' LOVE
in all of this. It's easy to be angry at boundaries, but parents
use them to show you love and keep you safe. You can harm
your relationship by not seeing how much your parents love
you and want to help you safely navigate to adulthood!*

*I know my parents love me by setting boundaries because . . .*

_____

_____

_____

_____

_____

And, despite all the potential harms, we have this promise of Jesus:

Surely I am with you always,
to the very end of the age.
(Matthew 28:20)

# Texting, Email, Social Media, Searching the Web— Are These a Few of Your Favorite Things?

## (Psst . . . do you have "internet addiction"?)

*Both Parents and Kids:*

There is debate over whether people can be addicted to the internet. At the time of this writing, there is no actual diagnosis code for internet addiction. Did you just tune out the words *diagnosis* and *code*?

Maybe you immediately thought of coding and gaming  design? You don't have to understand what the words mean—that's jargon/wording in the medical and insurance world. *What it means* is that the doctors haven't been able to decide if there is an actual disorder involving too much time on the internet. There are many reasons for this. You might spend hours researching a project or work entirely online for your job (dream job?), but that doesn't mean you are *addicted* to using the internet. It's really hard to figure out how many hours would be too many spent online before you suddenly become an "addict." You could be on a device *every day* for your job and never have an addiction. The internet is just what we might use to satisfy an addiction to do something else, like gambling or shopping (Konnikova).

133

*What do you think of when you hear the word <u>addiction</u>?*

Kid's response: _____

_____

_____

_____

_____

_____

Parents' response: _____

_____

_____

_____

_____

_____

When we think of addictions, we might think of things a person feels he or she NEEDS to do. In fact, it's probably something he or she **can't stop** doing. Some addictions involve substances (things). People will take the normal use of something to a level that becomes harmful or use a substance that is illegal. You may have thought of alcohol or drug abuse. Addictions can also be in our behaviors; the American Addictions Centers report some addictions involving food, gambling, exercise, or even shopping. While we all need food and have to shop at some point, these behaviors become *addictions* when a person continues eating or shopping *even though* the activities will hurt the person's health or life. The "addict" feels strongly pushed (compelled) toward the behavior and then later feels guilty (the food was more than was necessary and now hurts my health; the shopping puts me into more debt) (American Addictions Center). The intense needs begin in the brain, and at that moment, the person feels the need for the "hit" even though it will cause harm later. All addictions also share another connection: all are done to fill a need, but none ever satisfy past the initial "hit"—the bite of the brownie, the scratch-off ticket that *again* didn't win the lottery.

Does it really matter, though, if something has an official diagnosis? Does something <u>not</u> exist just because *we* can't figure it out or label it. You may never be able to explain nuclear fusion, but that doesn't mean it doesn't exist! If you have a rash on your arm that the doctor can't identify or treat *it is still a problem for you* (and is probably really annoying!). That doesn't mean the rash *isn't real* just because doctors can't identify it!

We already hinted that many people have an uncontrollable need to check a phone (remember Mark Love's story and how he created a box to keep him from continually checking his phone). Just because you check your phone a whole lot doesn't necessarily mean you have an internet addiction. However, therapist Sheryl Cowling, when asked about electronics use, explained, "Electronics can become addicting. If a parent notices that a child or teen is spending dramatically more time with their electronics and less and less time with family and friends, and/or becomes angry, irritable, or defiant when asked to put their electronics away, it may be time to consult a professional for guidance."

*Can you share a time you were angry or disagreed with your parents' decision (rules) about your cell phone or electronics time?*

*Kid's response:* _____

_____

_____

_____

_____

_____

*Parents' response:* _____

_____

_____

_____

_____

_____

The American Psychiatric Association's 📚 *Diagnostic and Statistical Manual* (or the DSM-5), the book that shows whether there is an actual written diagnosis for doctors and insurance, *has* included a section for "Internet Gaming Disorder." The APA is recommending research be done to decide if there should be an official disorder of being addicted to video games. Many of us have known or heard of someone who seems addicted to playing video games. It may seem like an exaggeration, but there are *real* people who have put themselves in danger or stopped doing normal things necessary for life (eating, sleeping, etc.) just to continue playing video games. So when does the once-in-a-while video gaming marathon become a full-blown problem? The signs are the same as they are with the other addictions or addictive behaviors: ignoring normal relationships (like spending time with parents, hint hint), ignoring health needs (sleeping, eating), and ignoring responsibilities of life (school, job, paying the bills, etc.) just to keep playing video games. One man, Ryan Van Cleave, wrote a book about his personal journey of video game addiction. As mentioned, part of what people like about texting/posting/gaming/surfing is being in control—face-to-face communication requires more work (and yet, more payoff as you build real relationships!). Van Cleave admits that gaming made him feel in control. Even though his real life had a wife, kids, and his dream job, he nearly threw it all away after 18 straight hours of gaming. Van Cleave nearly jumped off a bridge that day, but fortunately he did come back to reality (Lush). After that, Van Cleave began rebuilding *his life* instead of just another avatar. Some have not been so fortunate. There are sad stories of people neglecting themselves or others just to play an online game: a son shooting his parents when they tried to stop him from playing, people dying from extended periods of play, and parents neglecting an infant who actually died while the parents played video games (MacGregor).

*When is it too much and could be causing you to hurt yourself or others? How do you think these situations could be prevented?*

*Kid's response:* _____

_____

_____

_____

_____

_____

_____

*Parents' response:* _____

_____

_____

_____

_____

_____

Sadly, as sinful humans, we have the potential to use *nearly anything* to harm ourselves. Food, exercise, shopping, gaming, and the internet are all neutral things (not good or bad by themselves). Take any one of the listed things, and just add a human. The food is not a problem until a person eats too much or too little. These actions use things to bring a temporary high—which will never fill that need, will never satisfy in the long-term. Because the things we use (internet, food, etc.) are only a problem when people misuse them, it is hard for the professionals to figure out *how* or *whether* we can even create an internet addiction diagnosis.

Ikeepsafe.org helps parents and kids navigate the digital world and gives tips and tools to help identify a possible internet addiction. The site highlights a checklist from Dr. Kimberly Young, the Director of the Center for Internet Addiction Recovery, to help parents identify the potential warning signs in children of addictive internet use:

⚠ Loses track of time while online

⚠ Sacrifices needed hours of sleep to spend time online

⚠ Becomes agitated or angry when online time is interrupted

⚠ Checks email several times a day

⚠ Becomes irritable if not allowed access to the internet

⚠ Spends time online in place of homework or chores

⚠ Prefers to spend time online rather than with friends or family

⚠ Disobeys time limits that have been set for internet usage

⚠ Lies about amount of time spent online or "sneaks" online when no one is around

⚠ Forms new relationships with people he or she has met online

⚠ Seems preoccupied with getting back online when away from the computer

⚠ Loses interest in activities that were enjoyable before he or she had online access

⚠ Becomes irritable, moody, or depressed when not online (iKeepSafe) Reprinted with permission.

Before you suddenly decide, **"I'm an internet addict!"** know that *most people* will probably experience *some* of these symptoms at one time or another. Remember that Dr. Young noted these as "potential" warning signs. Being aware that a person *may* have a problem is always a part of *solving* or preventing a problem.

*Thoughts? Did anything on the list shock you? Which symptom(s) have you experienced before?*

*Kid's reaction:*_____

_____

_____

_____

_____

*Parents' reaction:*_____

_____

_____

_____

_____

One of the best things you can do if you are worried that *you* or *someone you know* may be addicted to his or her device(s) is to start the conversation. Talk about what you've learned and what you see that makes you concerned. Medical doctors can certainly help and advise whether professional treatment, either with a licensed counselor or more intensive treatment, is necessary. There are actually several treatment centers across the US. These centers are there specifically to help people whose lives and relationships are being hurt by constant media use. One such treatment facility, Outback Therapeutic Expeditions in Utah, takes patients to the rugged frontier, where they will learn to survive without the comforts of computers, family, or friends (Foran). Other facilities, such as reSTART, invite you to "restart your life, not your device" *(ReSTART Life)*. What many of these programs have in common is that they help patients develop other interests and skills to enjoy. Hopefully, people will turn to these interests instead of the easy and distracting "swipeability" of a device, or even scarier—turning to the phone as a coping tool to avoid life.

*Point to ponder: Are people avoiding getting out and having experiences that previous generations have had because they just sit on devices? (Looking at a picture of something rather than seeing it, hiking it, experiencing it?) Do you ever do that? Are we so easily distracted that we're missing out on life experiences?*

Kid's reaction:_____

_____

_____

_____

_____

_____

_____

Parents' reaction:_____

_____

_____

_____

_____

_____

_____

*Parents and Kids:.*

**Story Time:** Failure to thrive—this is a term given to infants who can't seem to gain weight, which then keeps them from thriving, or growing as they should. Although we don't usually use "failure to thrive" for other situations, it does apply at other times in life. When children head off to school (a new school, high school, or off to college), they are heading into new challenges and hurdles. The newness is often scary and full of anxiety, while being exciting at the same time. These are the times children (and parents) have butterflies in their stomachs and maybe some sweaty palms. Those reactions are *normal*. As crazy as it sounds, it is *normal* for people to have adrenaline rushes in these situations. *Will anyone give me the time of day, let alone sit with me? Will I find people like me?* These are scary moments that have been happening for centuries (and people have lived through them!). Today we have a new factor to living and thriving through these awkward and yet necessary growing pains: we have cell phones.

Recently, two mothers, unaware of each other's problems, told me about how they each had a son who decided to leave the school he was attending. The problem? Failure to thrive—not medically, but socially. Each boy had turned to the phone, contacting old friends on the phone or gaming, rather than connecting with new people.

The truth: It *is* hard to talk to people you don't know! It *is* hard to put yourself out there—in a group, at a cafeteria, in a new job. It *is* just plain hard. That *is* reality. It's been like this **for as long as people have existed** in a sinful world. But now when a person is afraid to talk to or approach a new group, he or she can just take out the phone. It's just so easy to ignore uncomfortable situations—just check in with the old friends, watch videos, or play games. And that may work for a while, but eventually old friends move on, or the devices can't actually give what we need—the human touch. As for the boys, both went home for the summer. One moved on to a completely new school the next year and started over new. The other went home and worked and has since gone back to take classes again. Lesson learned—get out there.

This is the reality: **face the awkward right away** or **face it later.** You can only hide or put things off for so long! Swallow hard, tuck the phone away, and start your future—*with* people.

*Do you see people avoiding people? Why is it so important to meet new people in new situations? What is the scariest part of that? (Do you think it gets easier?)*

*Kid's response:* _____

_____

_____

_____

*Thoughts on this for parents: How can you help prepare your child and give your child opportunities to become <u>independent</u> and <u>personable</u> (not hiding behind the phone)? What could you allow your child to do to increase his or her self-reliance AND show you trust your child to be more mature? (Make a purchase or a return at the store on their own, etc.) These are ways parents and kids grow closer—through the trust factor that "you can do this" and navigating the "ropes" toward maturity together.*

*Parents' response:* _____

_____

_____

_____

_____

Maybe you're thinking, "Sure, I need to help my child become more independent and learn to put himself out there, but how does that relate to internet addiction?" The reality is that we're becoming dependent on phones and devices for so much of our lives. You read the anecdote about the boys seeking the phone/devices instead of meeting people . . . because it was hard. The digital world makes it easier to avoid the things we don't want to face. And not only is the phone a distraction (go-to) for "what I don't want to do," it's being programmed to draw us in and keep us there. In fact, programmers study how we use phones and our reactions in order to purposefully make anything and everything about phones more addictive. In a *60 Minutes* interview about "brain hacking," Anderson Cooper talked to people who design and code phone apps. When prompted that there seems to be an addiction code (as in, how to program the phone to be more addictive), the programmer, Ramsay Brown, replied, "Yeah, that is the case. That since we've figured out, to some extent, how these pieces of the brain that handle addiction are working, people have figured out how to juice them further and how to bake that information into apps" (Cooper).

*What is it about your favorite apps that keeps you coming back for more?*

*Kid's response:* _____

_____

_____

_____

_____

*Parents' response:* _____

_____

_____

_____

_____

Ramsay Brown went on to explain: "You're part of a controlled set of experiments that are happening in real time across you and millions of other people"—like guinea pigs being observed (Cooper). The longer we stay online, the more information the companies gather about us.

*What do you think (or feel) about people watching and analyzing what you do online?*

*Kid's response:* _____

_____

_____

_____

*Parents' response:* _____

_____

_____

_____

At what cost is this happening? It would appear most of these things "cost" nothing—free app, anyone? Advertising companies doubled what they spent in 🗓️ two years—**31 billion**—just to show you their ads on social media (you know, those annoying ads off on the side of what you're really trying to look at 😊) (Cooper).

*These companies are seriously (31 billion?) invested in you being online. How do you feel about that?*

*Kid's response:* _____

_____

_____

_____

_____

_____

_____

*Parents' response:* _____

_____

_____

_____

_____

_____

_____

_____

*Although most of the online pastimes are "free," list some of the "costs" (ex: time, tempting an addiction?)*

*Kid's response:* _____

_____

_____

Parents' response: _____
_____
_____

Although you may never have an actual internet addiction, you may now view the whole digital industry in a different light. Even the simple online games are not really simple—they are backed by teams designing for addictiveness, watching how you use apps, and advertising with a vengeance. Parents, we need to help our children understand, as mentioned in the empathy section, that even though it might be easier to turn to the phone, the payoff for being with people *is* ultimately better!

And . . . don't forget that God goes with you through all this!

"Do not fear, for I am with you;
do not be dismayed, for I am your God.
I will strengthen you and help you;
I will uphold you
with my righteous right hand."
(Isaiah 41:10)

# Safety, Security, and Settings? Oh, My!

## (Prefer the Lions and Tigers? Don't Give Up Yet!)

*Parents (Kids, tag along):*

Very often I hear parents say, "My kids are *way* more advanced than I will ever be on computers, devices, the internet—all of that."

*Agree? Disagree? Why or why not?*

*Parents' response:* _____

_____

_____

_____

_____

You may feel digitally overwhelmed when you read magazine articles or internet titles such as, "Six-Year-Olds Outstrip Adults in Digital Understanding but Teens Lead the Way." Before we even dive into *that* arena, let's start with the basic building blocks of security and safety *(and, yes, you can do this!).*

## Building Block #1:

*Does my child know I love him or her? (How?)* _____

_____

_____

_____

*Do I often <u>tell</u> my child I love him or her?*_____

_____

_____

_____

**Story Time:** I love all of my students. Some definitely take more time and energy than others, but I really deeply love them <u>all</u>. One day after school, I had a student stay after to finish work before he could go to basketball practice. It saddened me to do this, but his mother and I were at our wits' end trying to help this extremely bright child complete work on time. As we walked to the classroom, I asked the child, "You know I'm only doing this because I love and care about you, right?"

He nodded and added, "Yes, because you tell us that you do all the time."

Children are listening. Maybe they're not always carrying through on the "what" you want them to do, or doing it how you'd like them to, *but they are listening.* There are days you may think you are spending more time rebuking and correcting than anything else. However, your children will know you love them if you are always *showing* and *telling* them that you do. That child's answer warmed my heart and encouraged me to continue showing that love in words and actions—*especially* when it's hard.

The first basic building block of safety and security is love and trust. That doesn't mean your relationship is suddenly just a walk in the park *(with fully choreographed dancing and music in the background?)* because you love and trust each other. However, when you get down to this base level, they know you toe the line *because* you love them.

## Building Block #2:

*Do you tell and remind your child that he or she can tell you <u>anything</u>? (And/or show this in other ways?)*_____

_____

_____

_____

It's not too late if you feel lacking in the "I'm available" depart-ment, but it is important to work on this. One of the best ways you can safeguard and offer security is by **being there.** If you are approachable, your child will feel able to come to you for help. This can be as easy as, "Hey, just so you know, you can tell me anything. I may not always be happy about it, but you are my child, and I will always love you and be there for you." Many situations spiral out of control because children are too afraid or embarrassed to tell a parent. That fact is a predator's dream. Many *big* issues can be fixed more easily and quickly if children feel safe telling a parent.

Parents, back to the earlier question, "Do you feel overwhelmed?" It seems so many parents think if they say out loud, *"I'm relatively clueless about the internet, computers, or social media,"* they have done their best and can sign off as being helpless. Be honest if you feel or at least wish it could be that way. The issue is that this child (whom you just declared you love and want to feel comfortable coming to you with anything) **is your responsibility.** Think about and pray over these words of Jesus: 📖 "See that you do not despise one of these little ones. For I tell you that their angels in heaven always see the face of my Father in heaven" (Matthew 18:10). God the Father in heaven never for a minute stops paying attention to your child or to the questions and concerns and day-to-day instructions of the angels that watch over your child. Any dangers to your child are a big deal to the heavenly Father. This child is a precious *gift* to you from him. Now, this child, the one you planned for and anticipated, needs **your** help and guidance. You would *never* allow your child to give up on math because it's suddenly hard in seventh grade. You'd study up, watch a tutorial or get a tutor to help explain what a parabola is. *You wouldn't just let it go.* Parents can't let it go on the digital front either. You love your child. If you are ill-prepared, you will study and learn. It's a good model for children to see that *they are loved so much* that you will take the time to understand and learn about the digital world in order to keep them safe. You aren't alone in this either. God goes with you in this. God is there as you pray for strength, and God is there to motivate you when this seems hard or scary. These children belong to God first—ask for his guidance:

"For it is God who works in you to will and to act in order to fulfill his good purpose," Philippians 2:13.

## Safety

*Parents and Kids*:

You've already taught children not to talk with strangers ("stranger danger!"). So much of the online world is about connecting people to other people (and sometimes, those people are strangers). Even the innocent games first and second graders are playing online have them connecting to other people. This is cute when you can find your classmates or cousins but **not so cute** when a creepy, middle-aged man is trying to get to know your first grader or "follow" your teenager on social media.

So teach about "stranger danger" again in digital world.

**"Be Aware of What You Share."** Anything that goes onto the World Wide Web has the potential to go anywhere in the world ( "Grandma Rule" extended).

For starters:

 If you don't want your child's full name out there, explain to him that he or she shouldn't use his full name for any usernames.

 If you don't want your address known, explain to him or her not to tell, write, or post pictures with your address.

*Brainstorm: What are things we want to be careful not to share online?*

*Parents and Kids:* _____

_____

_____

_____

_____

 It may sound like common sense, but don't share your passwords (except with your parents)! Internet security experts Amber Mac and Michael Bazzell recommend having children write their codes and passwords on paper and having parents keep a backup copy in case the child loses his. Although this seems "old school," they note that no hacker could steal your paper through the internet (Mac and Bazzell). Keeping a password private may **not** be hard if your child has a strong personality, but many children feel if a friend asks for it then they *need* to give it. It seems to start in elementary school with, "I want your snack," and morph into deeper and darker problems in the teenage years. The simple answer can start in grade school with, "My mom says I can't." (Parents don't mind taking the hit here.) Also, turn the tables from "You should give me your snacks/passwords, etc. *because we are friends*" to, *"Because* we are friends, you need to respect that I won't give it (whatever it is) to you. True friends don't bully or force." Older teens in relationships are often pressured to share passwords as a sign of trust and commitment—and sometimes in rebellion against those who say you shouldn't (Richtel). Unfortunately, when friends disagree or relationships turn sour, the damage starts on a digital playing field. The best advice: It's your password, and let's keep it that way!

*Do you feel comfortable saying no to friends? Have you seen friends pressured to share passwords (or even food, etc.)? What works when saying no?*

*Kid's response:* _____

_____

_____

_____

_____

*Advice? Parent response:* _____

_____

_____

_____

_____

How about devices—does anyone ask to use any of yours? If so, how did (or can) you keep them from having the device or knowing codes?

Kid's response: _____

_____

_____

_____

_____

Advice? Parent response: _____

_____

_____

_____

_____

## Passwords Continued

The Federal Trade Commission (FTC) has many guidelines to help parents and kids find their way through cyberspace and cyber security. They recommend that passwords use 10-12 characters, mixing letters and numbers, and not using predictable choices (birthdates, names, etc.). They also recommend NOT using the same password for different sites (if it's stolen someone could possibly then hack *everything* you use) and NOT sending information to *any company* asking for this information (the *real companies* wouldn't ask for that over email) (Federal Trade Commission). These same guidelines would apply for passcodes on phones and devices too.

What other information does your family want to be kept safe? (Like, don't post where we are until we are home from vacation, don't share personal family issues, etc.)

Kid's thoughts:_____

_____

_____

_____

_____

_____

*Parents' thoughts:*_____

_____

_____

_____

_____

_____

## Security and Settings

**Email and Internet** You're working to "be aware of what you share," but what about security issues? Keep devices updated, and only buy security protection from trustworthy companies. Do you need to talk about how, if something looks fishy (like an email or pop-up about winning money), it may possibly be phishy? Do you understand common phishing scams or when you can click a link versus when you should go directly to websites? Again, never give that personal information mentioned above without a parent giving the okay!

*Parents: Explain "phishy" emails/scams.*_____

_____

_____

_____

_____

_____

**Social Media** What about security in social media? It's impossible to cover all possible social media apps because the popularity of one versus another may change overnight! That being said, you can fight internet with internet. Parents, you will first need to know how to use a search engine (Google, Bing, etc.). Simply searching with the words "Parent help for _____" using the social media app's name usually takes you to the parent help page of that social media app or to a page designed to help parents understand that app. *You may need your child to help navigate* 😊, and then you can see how to set the security settings to whatever is the most private. You can give advice on whom to friend/allow to follow (i.e.

NOT anyone you don't know, and if they want to follow a certain celebrity, use it as an opportunity to talk about which ones are better choices and why). And know that all social media sites have you agree to their disclaimers (they really could legally own anything you post—check the fine print!). Many parents will actually join whatever app his or her child is on, and about half of parents require knowing their children's passwords (Pew Research Center, "Nearly Half of Parents").

*Are you familiar with the security settings of the social media your family uses?*

*Kid's response:* _____

_____

_____

_____

_____

*Parents' response:* _____

_____

_____

_____

_____

_____

Whether you actively have passwords to your child's information or simply watch as another user is a family's personal decision. Your family may choose to have an "unhackable" paper copy of the codes in a file (hint, a sheet of paper that can't be found in your computer) for just in case. As parents, you may allow your child the right to "keep" his codes with the understanding that a parent always has the right to look at anything a child does on the phone. My children with phones know that their dad can deactivate their phones with a few clicks on the phone carrier website . . . which, by the way, he has never had to do (i.e. they understand not to go over on data usage or do things that won't honor their parents).

Should your family have extra parental control apps? Ask friends, and research. A simple search of "Best parental controls for devices" will bring up lots of options. Some options are free, and new ones may pop up tomorrow, but do the research if you feel this is a good option for your family. Some apps will give the option to parents to see every message sent and every internet search done (include this in your search for an app if you want this option). Others are designed to protect users from harmful websites. Decide what level your family feels is best. My doctor has a device that allows her to see how much time her children spend on which sites and allows her to set limits and turn off capabilities remotely. You know your child(ren). Some children have amazing self-control and aren't lured by the addictiveness or what others are doing on phones; some are. You may have to tweak what you need as you go and individually per child.

*What kind of monitoring options might work for your family?*

*Kid's response:* _____

_____

_____

_____

_____

*Parents' response:* _____

_____

_____

_____

_____

Ephemeral images (pictures that disappear) can be a fun part of social media apps. They can also, however, give people a false sense of confidence when sending pictures one might not otherwise send. Those pictures can easily be saved by a screenshot. And for those who know what they are doing, ANY pictures **can** be found again. Ironically, **we** may never know how to find a favorite picture accidentally deleted, but a digitally savvy person can find what we don't want found. Again, the "Grandma Rule" obviously applies to ephemeral pictures (and really *all* pictures). But the thing to note here is that smartphones have Global Positioning Systems, or GPS, to help us navigate where we are. And, unless GPS is disabled, every time a picture is taken, it codes the GPS information into the picture. In other words, anyone who looks at the picture can find out where the picture was uploaded just by clicking onto the information associated with the picture (Birdsong). It may sound complicated to you, but by clicking on the picture it's like you've hand delivered your child's address to anyone who may want to find your child.

*What do you know and think about disappearing pictures and people finding people just by the information (GPS) attached to the picture?*

*Kid's response:* _____

_____

_____

_____

_____

*Parents' response:* _____

_____

_____

_____

_____

Posting frenzy, anyone? Some people feel it necessary to post each little detail of life (food, mood, etc.). Some people use options to "check-in" whenever they go anywhere. These options are not *necessarily unsafe,* but depending on what your child posts, or where he or she "checks-in," you may be allowing your child to lay a path for another person to stalk and know everything about your child (think of Hansel and Gretel's crumbs across the internet). Have a conversation about how much may be too much. Do we need to see pictures of all your meals or know everywhere you have been? Do you need to check-in *everywhere?*

How much is too much?

Kid's response: _____

_____

_____

_____

_____

Parents' response: _____

_____

_____

_____

_____

On a spiritual level, we have great safety and security through one easy passcode: J-E-S-U-S (and you *can* share this one). We are so blessed that we can trust God as our ultimate protection. We thank God for his protection as we fulfill the roles he's given us— "God is our refuge and strength, an ever-present help in trouble" (Psalm 46:1). God gave parents the role to protect and raise children. God gives children the role of obeying and honoring parents (with the promise of immeasurable blessings to follow Ephesians 3:20)! In these roles, we want to be good managers of what God's given us, to be safe and careful with what we have and do.

What are ways we show our thanks to God in the management of safety and security on devices?

Kid's response: _____

_____

_____

_____

Parents' response: _____

_____

_____

_____

How might we NOT be good managers (testing God—as in, God wants us to use all the gifts and knowledge he gives us to be proactive in life, so we should not passively just hope everything will be okay) through the safety and security of devices?

Kid's response: _____

_____

_____

_____

Parents' response: _____

_____

_____

_____

Parents, you may struggle with being a little lax, or maybe you worry over your child's device safety and security.

Kids and Parents: Mark where you think you fall on the line between "testing God" and "not trusting God enough."

**Testing God** ←————————————————————→ **Not Trusting God Enough**

In what ways might you be testing God or not trusting God enough with device safety and security?

Parents' response: _____

_____

_____

_____

_____

Kids, in what ways do you possibly test God or not trust God enough with internet safety and security?

Kid's response: _____

_____

_____

_____

The great thing is, Jesus goes with us through our shortfalls. We take our "lacks" to him, who is never lacking and never too busy—always safe and secure. We ask Jesus to forgive us and help us go forward in this sometimes challenging world.

*You might be a prayer warrior, or maybe that's a little unfamiliar to you. Write a short prayer to say <u>thank you to God for his safety</u> and <u>asking him to help and guide you to be safe and secure online</u>.*

Kid's prayer: Dear God, thank you _____

_____

_____

_____

_____

_____

Parents' prayer: Dear God, thank you _____

_____

_____

_____

_____

_____

Whatever you do, whether in word or deed,
do it all in the name of the Lord Jesus,
giving thanks to God the Father
through him.
(Colossians 3:17)

157

# The Darker Side of the Internet

**Parental Advisory Suggested**

*Parents:*

 "Every good and perfect gift is from above, coming down from the Father of the heavenly lights, who does not change like shifting shadows" (James 1:17). The internet and its many applications are such an amazing resource. It will keep morphing and changing. And yet, for each of those changing, improving blessings, we give thanks for a God who does not change. God always loves us unconditionally. This is an important truth and comfort to keep in the forefront as we dive into the reality of a sinful world:  "Be alert and of sober mind. Your enemy the devil prowls around like a roaring lion looking for someone to devour" (1 Peter 5:8). The devil—he's real, by the way, not just a fictitious character in horror movies—works to derail every gift of God. Since the beginning of time, even back in the Garden of Eden, the devil wanted to derail perfection. The same happens as the devil prowls the 21st century. Now evil has one more easy entry through which to enter into our lives—it's literally just a keystroke away.

The topics of sexting, sextortion, and pornography are uncomfortable and *seemingly* easier to just avoid. Unfortunately, we can't. If you allow your child *to have a device,* you have, at the very least, cracked the door for any of these problems to sneak into your child's life. You need to mentally and digitally prepare your child for this potential strike, this perversion of God's gifts.

**Story Time:** A child I know well convinced her dad to buy an exotic fruit at the grocery store. Harmless enough, right? Kudos for being fun, Dad! Not knowing how to actually slice and eat the dragon fruit, the teen does what most of us would do: she searches on a search engine. In a keystroke, the blink of an eye, she has opened a site that freezes her phone with pornographic pictures. Thankfully, she gave her dad the phone immediately— horrified. In the end, the phone problem was fixed, and they were able to find actual directions to cut and eat the fruit.

You may have had a similar circumstance. Why people feel the need to purposefully pervert God's gifts of marriage and sex and cause these cyber-pitfalls is beyond most of our rational minds. That being said, it does happen. The above situation turned out fine because the daughter was comfortable enough to ask for help (remember the previous chapter—establishing the trust that your child can come to you about anything?). Think of the complications that could have happened if she hadn't gone to Dad. She may have panicked and thought her dad would be angry. She may have thought *she* did something wrong to cause that, and because of that felt that she couldn't approach her dad. She may have solved the problem herself, but the graphic images would be unexplained, and she might have become curious and believed that this is normal behavior for adults. None of this happened, but it easily *could have* if there hadn't been open communication and trust between the daughter and her parents.

What do you think of this dragon fruit story?

Kid's reaction:_____

_____

_____

_____

_____

Parents' reaction:_____

_____

_____

_____

_____

_____

Catherine Steiner-Adair, a clinical psychologist, has studied the impact of digitalization on families and chronicles many people's stories along with her own findings in *The Big Disconnect*. She interviewed a fellow psychologist about his studies of pornography and boys. He told Steiner-Adair, "What is unnerving for them [parents] are the stories the boys told about seeing porn in the third or fourth grade. The average American child sees pornography now at eleven, and their parents are still not able to talk to them about it when they're thirteen or fourteen" (Steiner-Adair and Barker 184).

The story above, combined with the psychologist's studies, tells us something very important: We may not feel ready or qualified to have these conversations, but we *need* to. If you put a device into the hands of a child, you know he or she will at some time—in some internet mistype, some text—see something that is not appropriate. As parents, we owe it to our children to prepare them for this. We often ignore these subjects, yet the world we live in screams disturbing messages at them through many types of media all day long. We have a choice: talk to them, or allow popular culture to inform them.

God gave us these bodies. God also gave us other people, with whom we have different types of relationships. God also gave us heaven and time to live and spread his Word. As we have said before, we each have only so much time on earth—our "time of grace." During this time we have the opportunity to tell others about our amazing Savior and live in ways that say thank you to God. This chapter's topic is not even about new sins; these are just old sins with a modern makeover. In the Bible, Paul encouraged the Corinthians, who were struggling with the sexual sins of their time, "Do you not know that your bodies are temples of the Holy Spirit, who is in you, whom you have received from God? You are not your own; you were bought at a price. Therefore honor God with your bodies" (1 Corinthians 6:19,20). What a beautiful picture, that our bodies are "temples of the Holy Spirit." A temple is a holy place, a place to be in the presence of God, in the presence of eternity and heaven. When God made us his children, he moved right into our hearts, and now he lives in us. Our bodies are no longer just for shooting hoops or shopping or selfies. Our bodies are temples. When people come near us, they come to a holy place inhabited by God! We combat the ugly, discouraging, sinful attacks of this world by first of all remembering who we are: holy people loved by God so much that he himself came to die for us. "You were bought at a price." God "bought" us out of the devil's power, paying with his own blood at the cross. Realizing that we are so deeply loved and valued, we then value ourselves and our lives enough to tackle these problems. We then give thanks to God by teaching our children how we use our time and special relationships on earth.

Ready or not, here we come.

## Sexting

This includes any messages sent to another person involving nudity (nakedness) or semi-nudity. The first step is knowing and teaching children that as temples of the Holy Spirit, we honor God by honoring our bodies and keeping them private until marriage. That being said, we also want to find out what is happening that so many children are sexting so we can help our children navigate this time. It is important to understand why some think this practice is okay. Obviously, curiosity and hormones play a huge role, but many feel that it is harmless so long as you trust the person receiving the picture (Steiner-Adair and Barker 213). There is little thought of how the picture could later cause grief, regret, humiliation, and pain. There are many such stories—one story in *The Washington Post* is of "Maureen." Maureen was a typical seventh grader who thought a boy in class was showing interest because he liked her. He repeatedly asked for pictures, and finally she sent him one. She found out later that the picture of her in her underwear—that he *promised* he would *never* share—had become a school-wide game involving other girls he had also gotten pictures from. He had created a slideshow of the girls and freely showed them. That reckless, one-second picture, taken in her home bathroom, became the beginning of a horror story for her. She later ended up cutting herself and needed psychiatric help. At the time of the article, one of the other girls involved still hadn't recovered. As if all that wasn't bad enough—experiencing the hurt and shame—the sexting was also illegal. The *girls* and boy involved could be charged with child pornography (Contrera). Producing and/or having child pornography *may be illegal,* **even if a child created it.**

## Sextortion

This is similar to sexting; however, it usually involves being forced or bullied to share nude/partially nude photos, some kind of threat to show picture(s) to others, or even a threat to hurt someone if more photos/money aren't given (TeenSafe, "Sextortion"). TeenSafe also reports that many victims never report sextortion because of shame or fear no one will believe them. (This is why that trusting parent-child relationship of "I love you, and you can come to me about anything" is so important!). One of the most widely circulated sextortion stories is of a 13-year-old Canadian girl who flashed a topless picture on a video chat. When she refused to be blackmailed, the bully sent the video to her friends on Facebook. Three years later, in 2013, she released a video sharing her pain and suffering and then committed suicide (TeenSafe, "Sextortion").

None of this is easy to read, but it does bring home the importance of communicating, being available (for any topic!), educating our children (even when it's awkward), and practicing caution ("be aware before you share"—*anything* you post/send *anywhere* is out there!).

## Pornography

As stated above, many children are intentionally or accidentally seeing pornography as young as *third or fourth grade.* Steiner-Adair explains, "Children are learning a model of sexual intimacy and romance from pornography. All of them are ill-served" (Steiner-Adair and Barker 187). Pornography is a perversion of what God created for his people. In the perfection of the Garden of Eden, in Genesis, God wanted his people to be fruitful—to have children. God gave his people a mate, special relations, and the ability to reproduce.

God intended the intimate closeness of marriage, the closeness of a man and woman together for life, with no one separating them—God intended this closeness to be a gift and reflection of how very much he loves us. None of this is served in pornography. Pornography, like many of the digitally related problems, removes the emotion and real-person closeness (intimacy). It lowers people to becoming objects for curiosity or pleasure instead of **people** to love and partners in life. Looking at these pictures distorts (changes for the worse) children's views and can cause permanent psychological and spiritual damage. "There is no app for emotional intimacy. . . . To the extent that social media dominates a teen's time and attention, he or she is missing the kinds of conversation and face-to-face interactions that develop the relational skills for friendship and emotional intimacy" (Steiner-Adair and Barker 197). (For more Christian information on pornography, go to the website for Conquerors Through Christ: conquerorsthroughchrist.net)

*Parents:*

As you proceed, you have a lot of information to think about, and every family dynamic is different.

*Option 1: Have your child read the above information and journal thoughts/questions/comments below with your child.*

*Kid's response:* _____

_____

_____

_____

_____

_____

*Parents' response:* _____

_____

_____

_____

_____

_____

Option 2: Have your child read and fill out the breakdown of the topics below, and then proceed at your own pace. Or start here and see what your child knows, and fill out the section together.

Sexting (what it is/dangers):_____

_____

_____

_____

_____

_____

Sextortion (what it is/dangers):_____

_____

_____

_____

_____

_____

_____

Pornography (what it is/dangers):_____

_____

_____

_____

_____

_____

_____

Option 3: Proceed on your own in the space and/or revisit the information as needed.

_____

_____

_____

_____

_____

_____

## Wrap up:

Do you think kids realize they could possibly face charges as a criminal for sending and receiving indecent pictures? Did you realize how serious these crimes are for kids? How do we help kids be more careful (and realize they are hurting themselves and their parents and not honoring God)? What are your thoughts or reactions to all this?

Kid's response: _____

_____

_____

_____

_____

_____

Parents' response: _____

_____

_____

_____

_____

_____

**No!** In a world where we may be afraid of what is lurking one keystroke away—one download away—to tempt our children or what search may accidentally bring the ugliness of the world to your child's device, let us take comfort that God is here to be our support and guide. Let us, **"Seek the Lord while he may be found; call on him while he is near" (Isaiah 55:6).**

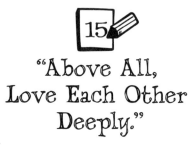

# "Above All,
# Love Each Other
# Deeply."

## 1 Peter 4:8

*Parents and Kids*

**Love.**

It's where the world began, why each of us exists, and why you are reading this page right now.

*How has your view of love changed while working through this book? (For instance, "I realize I love my phone, but it's different than how I love my parents because . . .").*

*Kid's response:* _____

_____

_____

_____

_____

_____

*Parents' response:* _____

_____

_____

_____

_____

**Value.**

We see value in each other and recognize that we don't fully know how much time God has given to us to be together. Devices are valuable tools, but they are not more valuable than the people in our lives. Devices easily connect, but they can also draw us away from people and things.

*In what ways do you value God more or differently than before?*

*Kid's response:* _____

_____

_____

_____

_____

_____

*Parents' response:* _____

_____

_____

_____

_____

_____

*In what ways do you value your child or parents differently now?*

*Kid's response:* _____

_____

_____

_____

_____

*Parents' response:* _____

_____

_____

_____

_____

### Be there.

Be *actually* present—emotionally and physically, your body, not the cropped and edited version! Support and bear one another's joys and sorrows.

"You can come to me with anything"—a comfort and promise to "be there" as children navigate.

*What ways have you found to become closer?*

Kid's response: _____

_____

_____

_____

_____

_____

Parents' response: _____

_____

_____

_____

_____

_____

### Be Aware of What You Share.

We represent ourselves, our family, and, most important, our God. What a tremendous honor and small *thank you* to the Savior of the world. Our managing of this technological gift is just one more way we show love and thanks to God!

*How have you changed in your view of what you share or habits of what you share?*

Kid's response: _____

_____

_____

_____

_____

_____

_____

_____

_____

_____

_____

Now to him who is able to do
immeasurably more
than all we ask or imagine,
according to his power
that is at work within us,
to him be glory . . .
for ever and ever!
Amen.
(Ephesians 3:20,21)

# Works Cited

American Academy of Pediatrics. "Children, Adolescents, and the Media." *American Academy of Pediatrics Policy Statement,* vol. 132, 2013, pediatrics.aappublications.org /content/pediatrics/ early/2013/10/24/peds.2013-2656.full.pdf. Accessed 20 June 2016.

American Addiction Centers. "Behavioral Addictions." *American Addiction Centers,* americanaddictioncenters.org/behavioral-addictions/. Accessed 24 Nov. 2016.

American Psychiatric Association. "Internet Gaming Disorder Fact Sheet." *American Psychiatric Association,* 2013, www.psychiatry.org/ psychiatrists/practice/dsm/educational-resources/dsm-5-fact-sheets. Accessed 25 Nov. 2016.

Arango, Alejandro. "A Parental Wake-Up Call: Time to Gain Control of Kids' Online Activity." *Family Online Safety Institute,* 7 Nov. 2016, www.fosi.org/good-digital-parenting/parental-wake-call-time-gain-control-kids-online-activity/. Accessed 20 Dec. 2016.

Birdsong, Toni. "How to Turn Off GPS on Your Child's Phone." *Securing Tomorrow. Today.* McAfee, 20 Aug. 2013, securingtomorrow.mcafee. com/consumer/family-safety/how-to-turn-off-gps-on-your-childs-phone/. Accessed 20 Dec. 2016.

Brown, Graham D. "100 Youth Market Statistics." *Total Youth Research,* www.totalyouthresearch.com/12-statistics-gen-y-privacy/. Accessed 29 Oct. 2016.

Cohen, Elizabeth. "Does Life Online Give You 'Popcorn Brain'?" CNN, 23 June 2011, www.cnn.com/2011/HEALTH/06/23/tech.popcorn.brain. ep/index.html. Accessed 25 Nov. 2016.

Contrera, Jessica. "And Everyone Saw It." Washington Post, 6 Sept. 2016, www.washingtonpost.com/sf/style/2016/09/06/ the-sext-was-meant-to-impress-him-instead-it-nearly-destroyed-her/?utm_term=.567c1402981c. Accessed 10 Sept. 2016.

Cooper, Anderson. "What is 'Brain Hacking'? Tech Insiders on Why You Should Care." Interview with Ramsay Brown. 60 Minutes. CBS News, 9 Apr. 2017, www.cbsnews.com/news/ brain-hacking-tech-insiders-60-minutes/. Accessed 14 Apr. 2017.

Cowling, Sheryl. LCSW, BCPCC, BCETS. Personal Interview. 20 Oct. 2016.

Curry, Candice. "I Thought Snapchat Was Ruining My Teen—But When She Landed in the ER, the Truth Came Out." For Every Mom, foreverymom.com/mom-gold/i-thought-snapchat-was-ruining-my-teen-but-when-she-landed-in-the-er-the-truth-came-out/. Accessed 27 May 2016.

Davidson, Jacob. "The 7 Social Media Mistakes Most Likely to Cost You a Job." Time, 16 Oct. 2014, time.com/money/3510967/jobvite-social-media-profiles-job-applicants/. Accessed 19 Dec. 2016.

Davis, Susan. "Is Your Child Ready for a Cell Phone?" WebMD, 2012, www.webmd.com/parenting/features/children-and-cell-phones#1. Accessed 16 Aug. 2016.

Federal Trade Commission. "The Protection Connection." Consumer Information. Federal TradeCommission, Aug. 2011, www.consumer.ftc. gov/articles/0033c-protection-connection. Accessed 20 Dec. 2016.

Ferman, Risa. "What Are Your Kids Really Doing on Their Cell Phones and How Can You Keep Them Safe?" Huffington Post, 3 Apr. 2013, www.huffingtonpost.com/risa-ferman/what-are-your-kids-really_b_3007504.html. Accessed 11 Oct. 2015.

"FOMO: This is the Best Way to Overcome Fear of Missing Out." Bakadesuyo.com, 2016, www.bakadesuyo.com/2016/06/fomo/. Accessed 10 June 2016.

Foran, Clare. "The Rise of the Internet Addiction Industry." The Atlantic, 5 Nov. 2015, www.theatlantic.com/technology/ archive/2015/11/the-rise-of-the-internet-addiction-industry/414031/. Accessed 25 Nov. 2016.

Foresters Financial. TechTimeOut. Foresters Financial, techtimeout.com. Accessed 22 Nov. 2016.

Gross, Gail. "Teens and Technology: Managing Cell Phone Usage." Huffington Post, 21 Apr. 2014, www.huffingtonpost.com/dr-gail-gross/teens-and-technology-managing-cell-phone-usage_b_5187412. html. Accessed 6 Feb. 2016.

Hill, Catey. "Millennials engage with their smartphones more than they do actual humans." MarketWatch, 21 June, 2016, www.marketwatch. com/story/millennials-engage-with-their-smartphones-more-than-they-do-actual-humans-2016-06-21. Accessed 21 Nov. 2016.

Homayan, Ana. "The Secret Social Media Lives of Teenagers." New York Times, 7 June 2017, www.nytimes.com/2017/06/07/well/family/the-secret-social-media-lives-of-teenagers.html. Accessed 3 July 2017.

iKeepSafe. "Too Much Time Online." iKeepSafe, ikeepsafe.org/be-a-pro/ balance/too-much-time-online/. Accessed 11 June 2016.

Jackson, Eric. "The 25 Biggest Regrets in Life. What Are Yours?" Forbes, 18 Oct. 2012, www.forbes.com/sites/ericjackson/2012/10/18/the-25-biggest-regrets-in-life-what-are-yours/#346595ae6488. Accessed 7 July 2016.

Konnikova, Maria. "Is Internet Addiction a Real Thing?" The New Yorker, 26 Nov. 2014, www.newyorker.com/science/maria-konnikova/ internet-addiction-real-thing. Accessed 23 Nov. 2016.

Lenhart, Amanda. "Cell Phones and American Adults." Pew Research Center, 2 Sept. 2010, www.pewinternet.org/2010/09/02/cell-phones-and-american-adults/. Accessed 15 Aug. 2016.

Lenhart, Amanda, et al. "Teens, Kindness and Cruelty on Social Network Sites." Pew Research Center, 9 Nov. 2011, www.pewinternet.org/2011/11/09/teens-kindness-and-cruelty-on-social-network-sites/. Accessed 4 July 2017.

Love, Mark. "The Be Present Box." Unfinished. Mark Love Furniture, 13 July 2013, marklovefurniture.com/blog/2013/07/13/the-be-present-box/. Accessed 12 June 2016.

Ludden, Jennifer. "Teen Texting Soars; Will Social Skills Suffer?" NPR, 20 Apr. 2010, www.npr.org/templates/story/story.php?storyId=126117811. Accessed 22 Aug. 2016.

Lush, Tamara. "At War with the World of Warcraft: An Addict Tells His Story." The Guardian, 29 Aug 2011, www.theguardian.com/technology/2011/aug/29/world-of-warcraft-video-game-addict. Accessed 25 Nov. 2016.

Mac, Amber, and Michael Bazzell. Outsmarting Your Kids Online: A Safety Handbook for Overwhelmed Parents. Edited by Y. Varallo and L. Killian, 2016.

MacGregor, Luke. "Digital Age Overload: 'Internet Addiction' to be Classified as Mental Illness." RT, 1 Oct. 2012, www.rt.com/news/internet-use-mental-illness-389/. Accessed 27 Nov. 2016.

McAffee. "70% of Teens Hide Their Online Behavior from Their Parents, McAfee Reveals What U.S. Teens are Really Doing Online, and How Little Their Parents Actually Know." McAffee, 25 June 2012, www.mcafee.com/us/about/news/2012/q2/20120625-01.aspx. Accessed 29 Oct. 2016.

Misra, Shalini, et al. "The iPhone Effect: The Quality of In-Person Social Interactions in the Presence of Mobile Devices." Environment and Behavior, vol. 48, no. 2, 2016, pp. 275 298, https://doi.org/10.1177/0013916514539755. Accessed 23 Nov. 2016.

Natanson, Hannah. "Harvard Rescinds Acceptances for At Least Ten Students for Obscene Memes." The Harvard Crimson, 5 June 2017, www.thecrimson.com/article/2017/6/5/ 2021-offers-rescinded-memes/. Accessed 4 July 2017.

National Institute of Mental Health. "The Teen Brain: Still Under Construction." National Institute of Mental Health. U.S. Department of Health and Human Services, 2011, infocenter.nimh.nih.gov/pubstatic/NIH%2011-4929/NIH%2011-4929.pdf. Accessed 2 June 2016.

National School Safety and Security Services. "Cell Phones and Text Messaging in Schools." National School Safety and Security Services, www.schoolsecurity.org/trends/cell-phones-and-text-messaging-in-schools/. Accessed 9 Aug. 2016.

Pew Research Center. "Mobile Fact sheet." Pew Research Center, 22 Nov. 2013, www.pewinternet.org/fact-sheet/mobile/. Accessed 26 Nov. 2016.

Pew Research Center. "Nearly Half of Parents Know Their Teen's Email Password; Roughly a Third Know Teen's Social Media Password." Pew Research Center, 6 Jan. 2016, www.pewinternet.org/2016/01/07/parents-teens-and-digital-monitoring/pi_2016-01-07_parents-teens-digital-monitoring_1-04/. Accessed 20 Dec. 2016.

PrepScholar. "Harvard Requirements for Admission." PrepScholar, www.prepscholar.com/sat/s/colleges/Harvard-admission-requirements. Accessed 3 July 2017.

Prooday, Victoria. "Why Are Our Children so Bored at School, Cannot Concentrate, Get Easily Frustrated and Have No Friends?" YourOT, 16 May 2016, yourot.com/parenting-club/2016/5/16/why-our-children-are-so-bored-at-school-cant-wait-and-get-so-easily-frustrated. Accessed 29 May 2016.

ReSTART Life. www.netaddictionrecovery.com/. Accessed 27 Nov. 2016.

Richtel, Matt. "Young, in Love and Sharing Everything, Including a Password." The New York Times, 17 Jan. 2012, www.nytimes.com/2012/01/18/us/teenagers-sharing-passwords-as-show-of-affection.html. Accessed 20 Dec. 2016.

Rideout, Victoria J., et al. "Generation M2: Media in the Lives of 8- to 18-Year-Olds." The Henry J. Kaiser Family Foundation, 20 Jan. 2010, kaiserfamilyfoundation.files. wordpress.com/2013/04/8010.pdf. Accessed 10 Aug. 2016.

Rowan, Chris. "10 Reasons Why Handheld Devices Should Be Banned for Children Under the Age of 12." The Huffington Post, 6 Mar. 2014, www.huffingtonpost.com/cris-rowan/10-reasons-why-handheld-devices-should-be-banned_b_4899218.html. Accessed 10 Aug. 2016.

Sedghi, Ami. "Six-year-olds outstrip adults in digital understanding but teens lead the way." The Guardian, 7 Aug. 2014, www.theguardian.com/news/datablog/2014/aug/07/six-year-olds-outstrip-adults-in-digital-understand-but-teenagers-lead-the-way. Accessed 24 Nov. 2016.

Smith, T., et al. "2010 Survey on Cell Phone Use While Performing Cardiopulmonary Bypass." Perfusion, vol. 26, no. 5, 2011, pp. 375-380, https://doi.org/10.1177/0267659111409969. Accessed 23 Nov. 2016.

Steiner-Adair, Catherine, and Teresa H. Barker. The Big Disconnect: Protecting Childhood and Family Relationships in the Digital Age. HarperCollins Publishers, 2013.

Stopbullying.gov. U.S. Department of Health and Human Services, www.stopbullying.gov. Accessed 9 Aug. 2016.

Sui, Linda. "44% of World Population Will Own Smartphones in 2017." Strategy Analytics, 21 Dec. 2016, www.strategyanalytics. com/strategy-analytics/blogs/devices/smartphones / smart-phones/2016/12/21/44-of-world-population-will-own-smartphones-in-2017#. Accessed 19 June 2017.

TeenSafe. "Sextortion: What Parents Need to Know." TeenSafe, 5 Dec. 2016, www.teensafe.com/blog/sextortion-parents-need-know/. Accessed 21 Dec. 2016.

TeenSafe. "The TeenSafe Parenting Guide to Tech Safety." TeenSafe, 24 Nov. 2014, www.teensafe.com/blog/teensafe-parenting-guide-tech-safety. Accessed 22 Dec. 2016.

The Henry J. Kaiser Family Foundation. "Daily Media Use Among Children and Teens Up Dramatically From Five Years Ago." The Henry J. Kaiser Family Foundation, 20 Jan. 2010, www.kff.org/ disparities-policy/press-release/daily-media-use-among-children-and-teens-up-dramatically-from-five-years-ago/. Accessed 11 Oct. 2015.

Turkle, Sherry. Reclaiming Conversation: The Power of Talk in a Digital Age. Penguin Publishing Group, 2016.

USA.gov. "Online Safety." USA.gov, www.usa.gov/online-safety. Accessed 9 Aug. 2016.

Vecchione, Glen. Science Facts. Sterling Publishing, 2007.

Wilson, Timothy D., et al. "Just Think: The Challenges of the Disengaged Mind." Science, vol. 345, no. 6192, 2014, pp. 75-77. https://doi.org/10.1126/science.1250830.

Wolpert, Stuart. "In Our Digital World, Are Young People Losing the Ability to Read Emotions?" UCLA Newsroom. UCLA, 21 Aug. 2014, newsroom.ucla.edu/releases/in-our-digital-world-are-young-people-losing-the-ability-to-read-emotions#tab-2. Accessed 29 Oct. 2016.

Zurbriggen, Eileen, et al. "Report of the APA Task Force on the Sexualization of Girls." American Psychological Association, 2007, www.apa.org/pi/women/programs/girls/report-full.pdf.